PATH PUZZLES

Easy to Pick Up. Hard to Put Down.

For carrie.
Get Path-o-Logical!

by Rod Kimball

Cover and interior design by Lauren Hom
http://www.laurennicolehom.com/

For more on Path Puzzles, visit:
http://www.pathpuzzles.com/

ISBN 978-0-578-12732-3

2nd edition

For Dad, who showed us that it's all puzzles.

Thank You...

To Tom Cutrofello for puzzle testing and encouragement, Stuart Haber for puzzle testing and instruction honing, Mark Hurst for not letting me use my self-designed cover, Lauren Hom for her design savvy and coaching, Mark Ettinger for giving it a comprehensivist look-see, Fritz Grobe for many of the differences between the 1st and 2nd edition, George Hart for getting me to shoot for a high level of quality in the puzzles, Viveca Gardiner for editing expertise, Wren Schultz for the honing of instructions and for Troothpicks, Francis Heaney for the benefit of his experience in many aspects of puzzle book creation, Zev Eisenberg for helping me to think big-picture, Kai, Denise, Alan and Brett Kuehner for puzzle testing and feedback on instructions, and to Emily Cornelius for being Emily Cornelius.

Contents

CAUTION!

Soon you will find yourself at the edge of a room filled with hidden danger! Your only option is to find your way to the other side. The floor appears solid but only a crooked, narrow path will bear you across. All the rest is as flimsy as paper. Can you reach the other side without falling through?

Your only guidance is a map with some clues regarding the location of the path you must walk to get out. The information seems inadequate, but it's all there is between you and falling...

Welcome to Path Puzzling!

Each puzzle is a map with clues that will help you find your way across a grid. At the edges of the grid are two or more openings. A path goes from one opening to another by winding its way from one cell to the next -- up, down, left or right, but not diagonally. (A "cell" is one of the squares in the grid.) The path may not go through any cell more than once. For each puzzle, there is only one path through the grid. Your job is to get from edge to edge by finding the path.

The numbers outlying the grid tell how many cells the path goes through in the corresponding row or column. For example the number 2 to the right of the grid below refers to the two shaded cells in the top row.

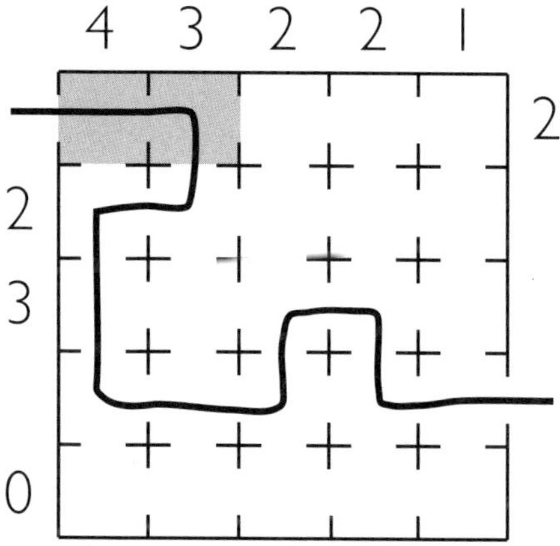

Sometimes, a number will seem to be missing. Nonetheless, part of the path may be in that row or column.

Very important: Use a pencil!

Rules for Special Situations

Multiple openings.

Sometimes, there will be more than two openings on the edges of the grid. Only two of them are used. All others are false and will not work as part of the solution. Whenever a puzzle has more than two openings, this symbol will alert you:

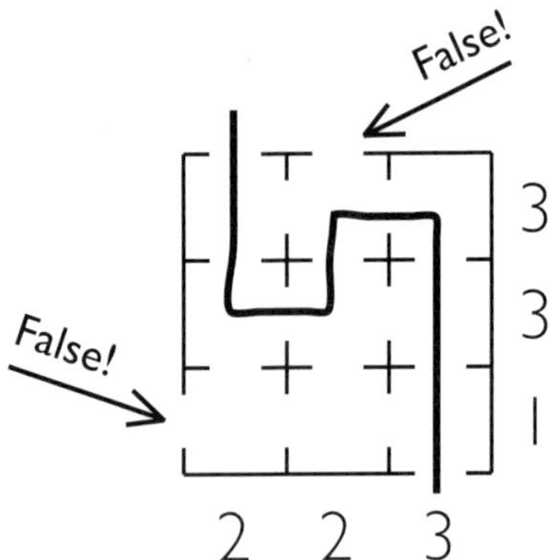

Numbers counting more than one row or column.

Sometimes, a number will be adjacent to more than one row and/or column. This number is the total count from all rows and columns it is adjacent to.

In this case, the 4 is the total number of cells occupied by the path in the row to the right of the 4 and the column below.

The 6 is the tally from the column above, the column below, and the row to the right.

The 8 is the tally from the columns above and below and the rows to the left and right.

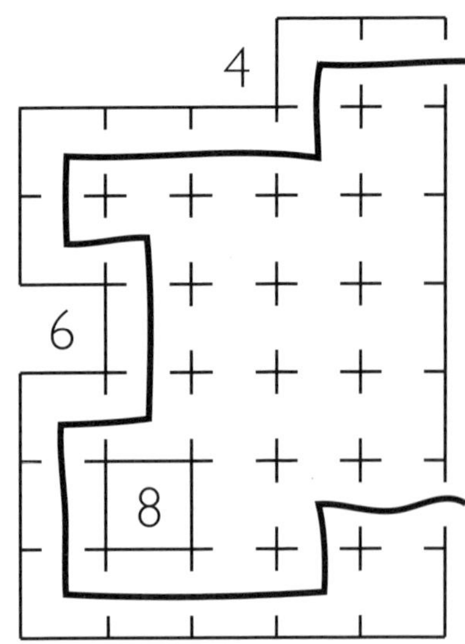

Interrupted rows or columns.

Sometimes, a row or column will be interrupted by a space which is not part of the grid where the path can go. This happens when the puzzle is of an irregular shape or when there is a number embedded in the grid. A few examples are shown in grey below.

In these cases, the numbers only count the uninterrupted rows or columns immediately adjacent to them.

Keep in mind that a number embedded in the grid interrupts both the row and column it is in.

Check out the numbers below to make sure you know what's being counted and what's not.

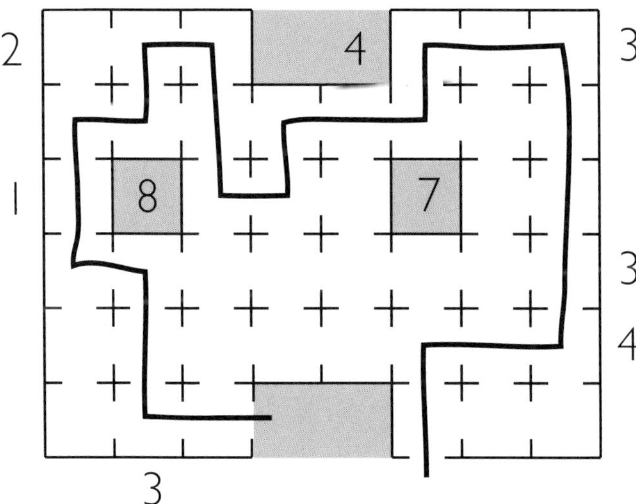

Tips for Solving

(Feel free to skip this part, but if you hit a snag, you may find it helpful.)

First, a walk-through guide for solving a simple path puzzle.

As you're figuring out how a path goes through a grid, it will be helpful to have a system for showing yourself what you've already learned about where it goes and does not go.

If you know how the path goes through a given cell, draw a line to show this. A good place to start is at the openings where the path enters and exits the grid. (Careful! Sometimes, there will be more than two openings on the edge of the grid, and you'll have to figure out which ones will work.)

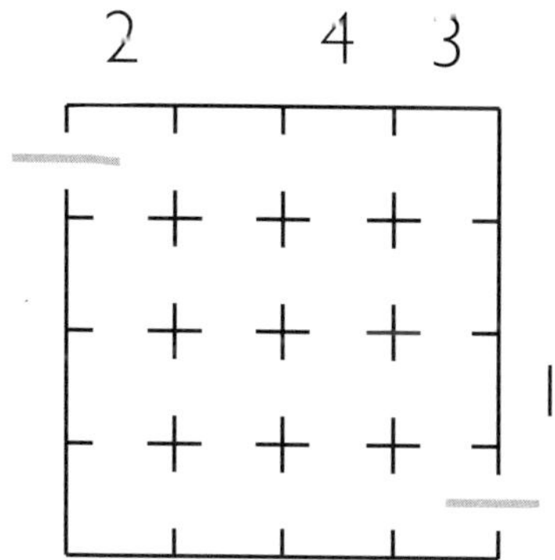

Now let's look at the numbers. The number 4 in this puzzle tells us that all four of the cells below it have the path running through them but it doesn't provide any information about how it does so. In cases like this, it is helpful to show that the path occupies certain cells even though you don't know how it enters or exits them. The symbol I use for this is a dot. Of course, you should feel free to use whatever works for you.

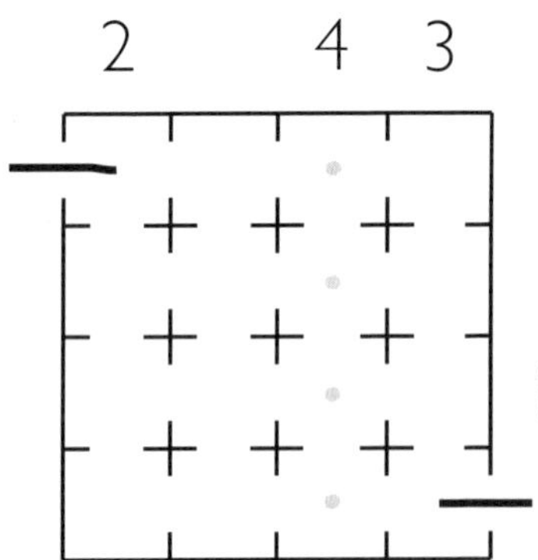

Now that we've established that the path goes through all the cells below the 4, we can see that the 1 on the right side of the puzzle is satisfied. Since the requirement of the 1 is fulfilled, we may not place the path in any more of the cells in the row next to the 1. To show that these cells are no longer available, let's X them out.

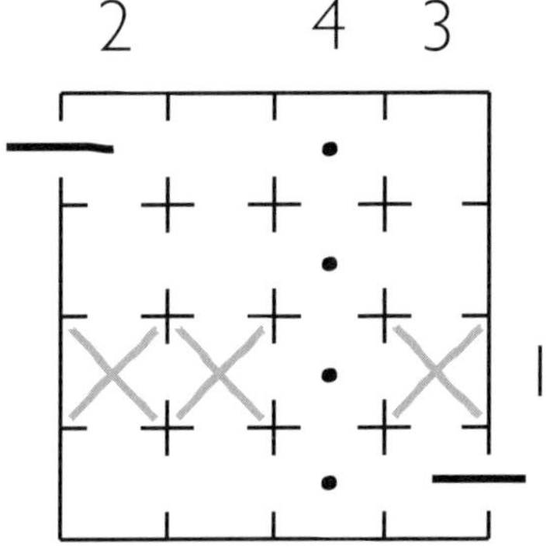

Now that we've discovered where the path can not go, we can see that there are only two unoccupied cells left available in the rightmost column. The path must go through both of them in addition to the one at the bottom of the column to satisfy the 3, so we can place dots in those cells.

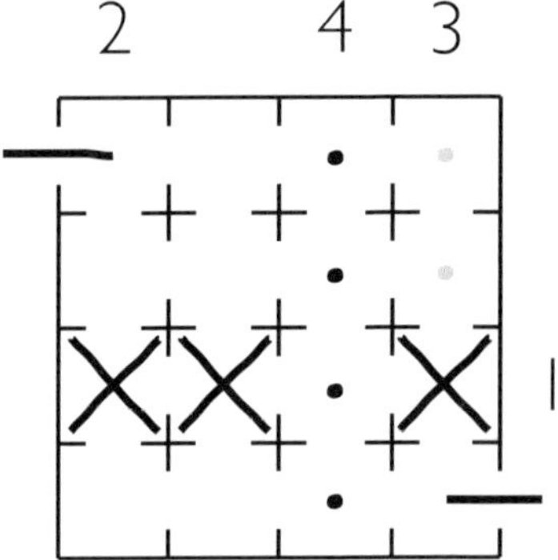

For every cell the path occupies, it needs a way in and a way out. With this in mind, we can see that the cell in the lower left corner is a dead end. Furthermore, if we can't go through that cell, we can't go through the cell next to it either. To show that we won't be using those cells, X them out.

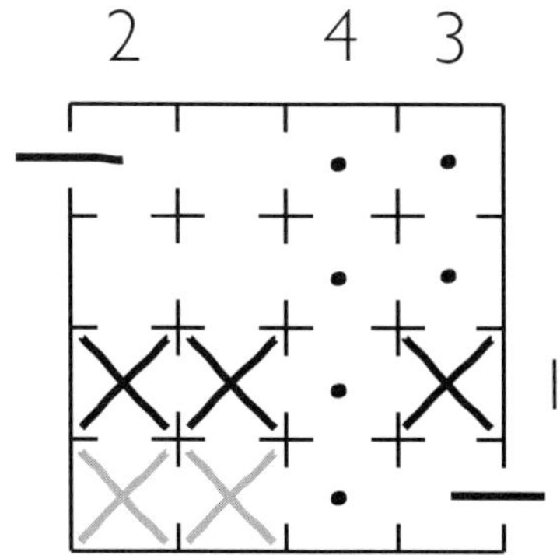

Most of the cells that now have dots in them have only two adjacent cells left available, so the path can pass through them in only one way. See if you can connect some of the path together by drawing a line through those cells. This will make it easier to see what to do next. The process has been started for you.

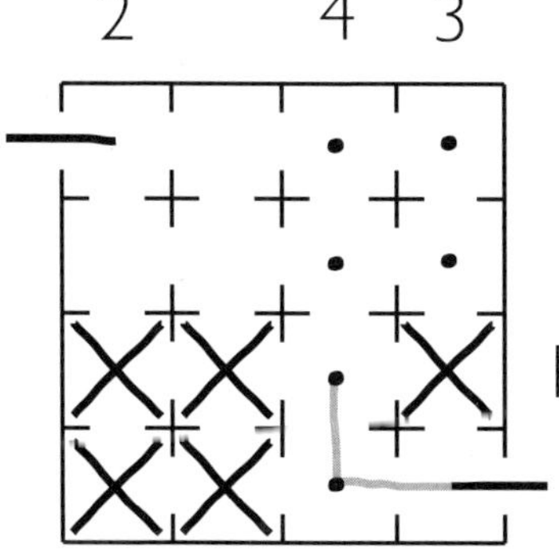

Before turning the page, try to figure out how the path gets through all the cells it occupies. (It will end up occupying more cells than the ones we've marked.)

Voilà! This is the only way through the grid.

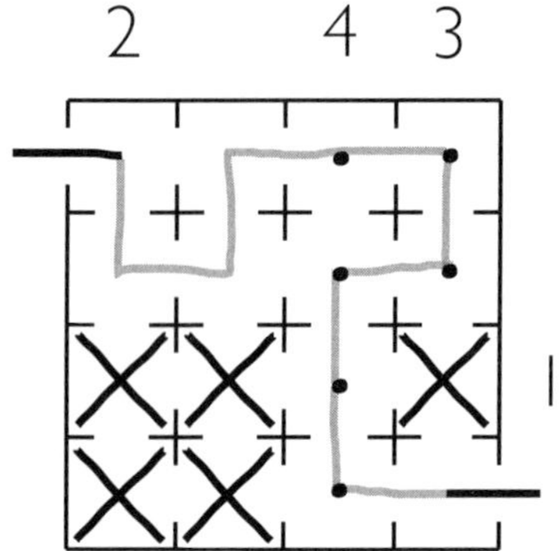

Now you're ready to solve many of the puzzles in this book.

Advanced Technique

As you progress to the more difficult puzzles in this book, more advanced techniques will become very helpful. One such technique is called "Proof by Contradiction". Most of the time, this method will not be necessary, but if you get stuck, it may come in handy.

Usually you'll be trying to prove something that seems likely—that the path goes through a particular cell or that it does not go through a particular cell. You will find it is often easier to prove these things by showing that the *opposite* case *cannot* be true.

In the puzzle below, the numbers tell us that we have both a column and a row with four of their five cells occupied by the path. It seems highly likely that the cell where this column and row intersect would contain a segment of the path. Let's put a dot there as something to try out.

By the way, it is important to have a way to keep track of which of your symbols represent something you've already figured out for sure and which ones are for an idea you're just trying out. I use a heavy, dark pencil stroke for when I'm certain and a light stroke for when I'm not. (In this explanation, the lightest markings are used for whatever is new in each successive step.)

I also like to put a circle around the particular hypothesis I'm testing. Later, when the hypothesis and all of its consequences are drawn in, the circle is how I remember which pencil mark represents the question I'm trying to answer.

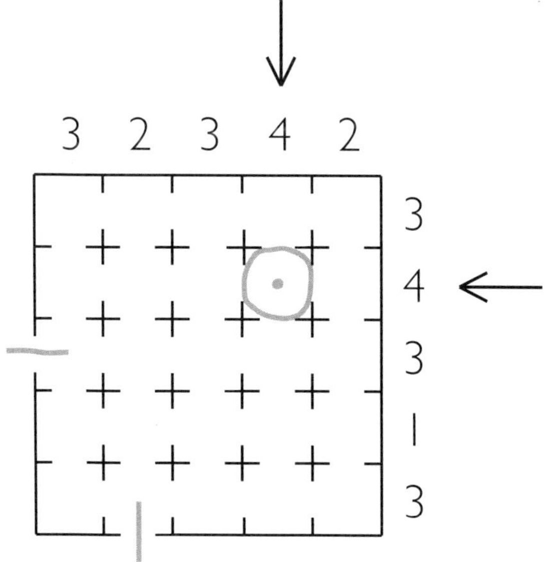

Having placed the dot, what do we do next? The hypothesis that the path goes through that spot has not made the next step any easier to see. Furthermore, we haven't actually proven that the path goes through that cell, and it's hard to know how to proceed, knowing that what we have so far might not be right. We could try adding another likely-looking assumption, but doing this only compounds the uncertainty. Sooner or later, one of these assumptions is going to be incorrect and it's going to be very difficult to know which one.

We won't be able to complete the path and we won't know why.

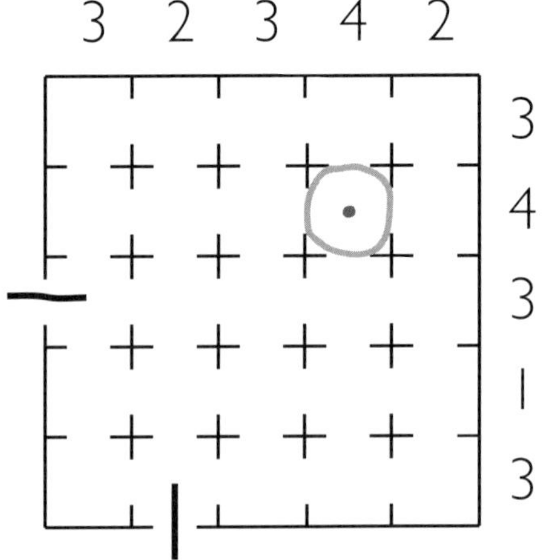

Now let's back up and see what happens if we propose that the path *does not* pass through that cell. To do this, we erase the dot and put an X there instead.

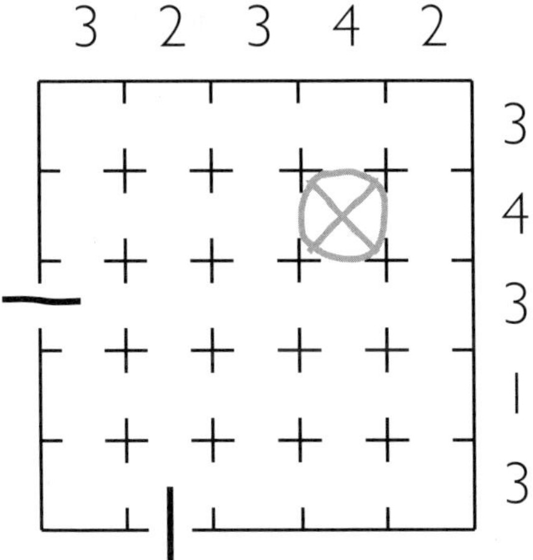

Immediately, consequences emerge. First off, there are only four cells left available in both the row and the column with the 4s at the ends. Let's fill them all up with dots representing pieces of the path.

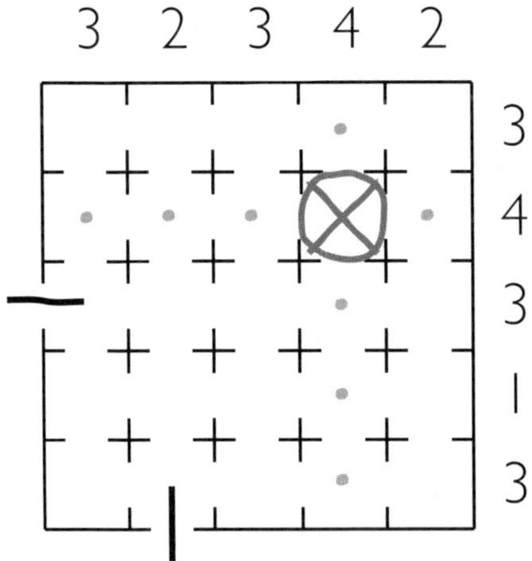

Now there are dots above and to the right of the 'X'. The result of the 'X' being there is that the path must go around it.

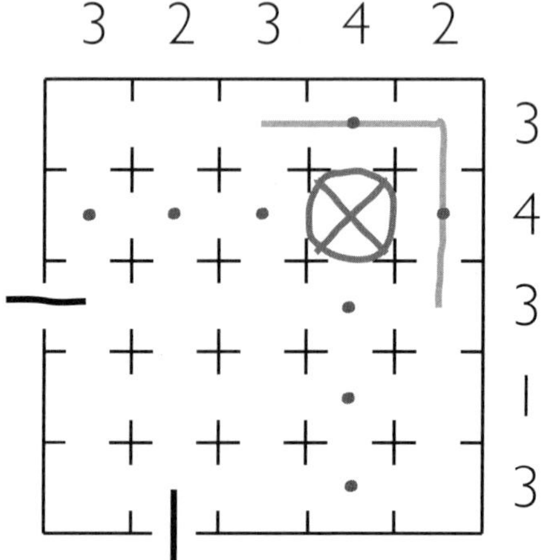

Having drawn the path around the X, we can see that it requires three cells in the rightmost column. Do you see the problem? Using three cells is in conflict with the 2 at the top of the column! Our proposition that the path does not go through the cell with the 'X' in it has forced the path to be in a place where it cannot be. Therefore, our proposition is incorrect. The only other option is that the path *does* run through that cell. This is no longer an assumption. We have actually proven it by contradiction and we can proceed knowing that we are on solid ground.

Wondering why it works this way? Picture yourself with a group of children. If you state that 2 plus 2 equals 4, you'll get nods and funny looks and they'll probably wonder why you're mentioning it. On the other hand, if you insist that 2 plus 2 equals 5, you're likely to get lots of lively conversation until you back down. As a general rule, incorrect information tends to draw more attention to itself than correct information.

Now you can go back to the first diagram in this explanation and solve the puzzle knowing that the path goes through that cell.

The journey of a thousand miles begins with one step.

Lao Tzu

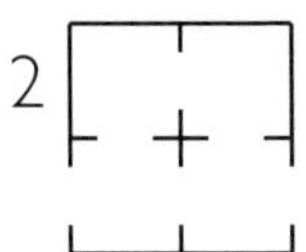

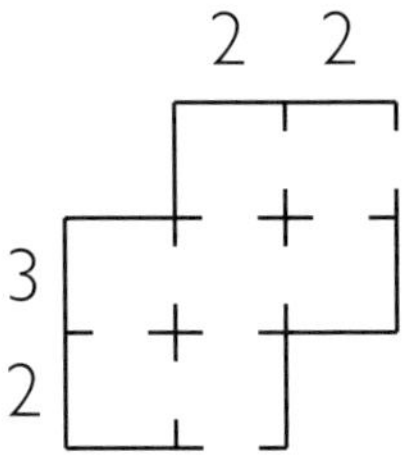

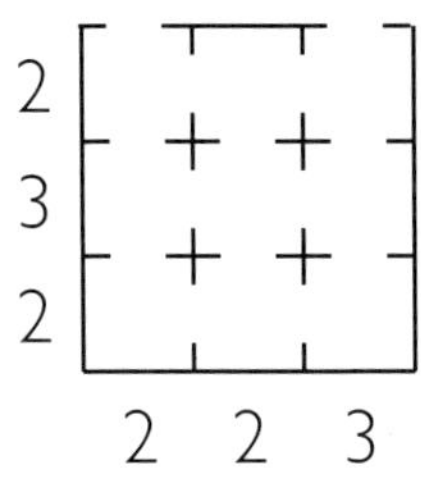

Solutions on page 89

1

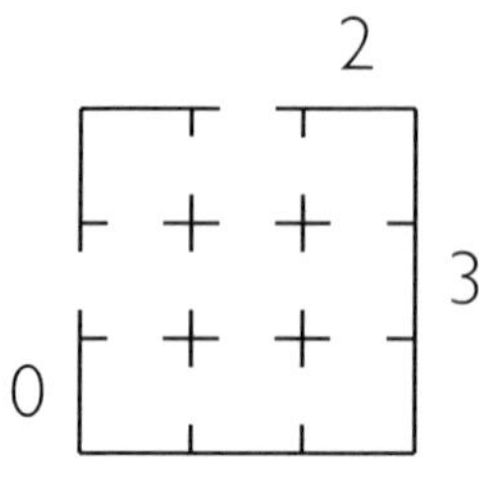

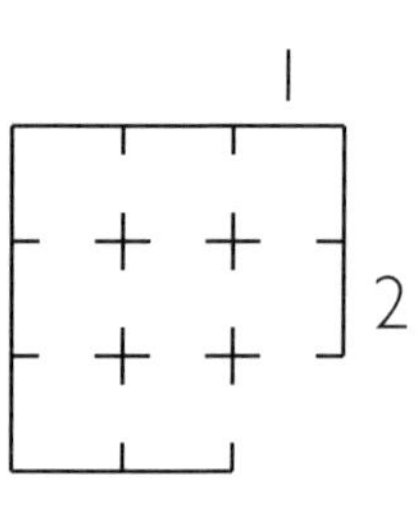

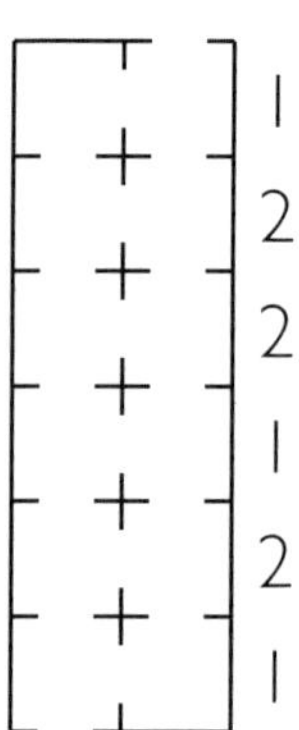

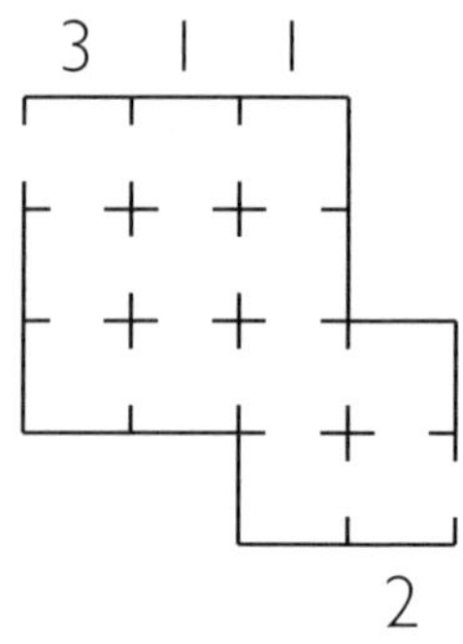

Solutions on page 89

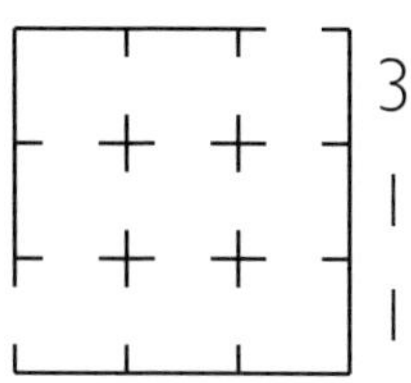

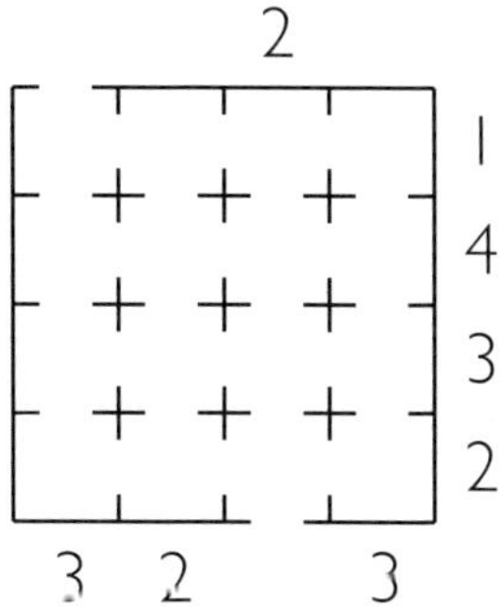

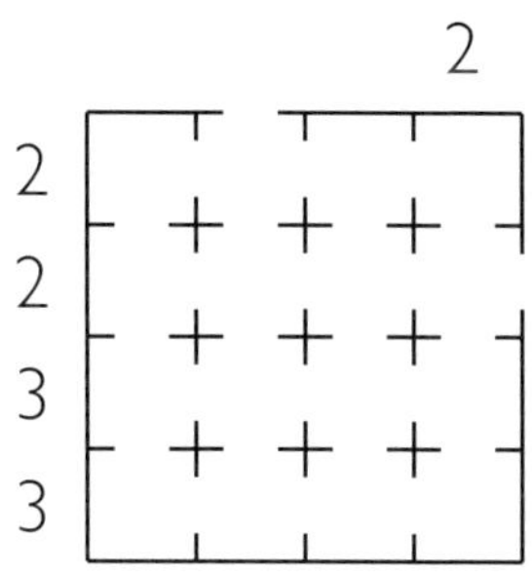

Solutions on page 89

A straight path never leads anywhere except to the objective.

Andre Gide

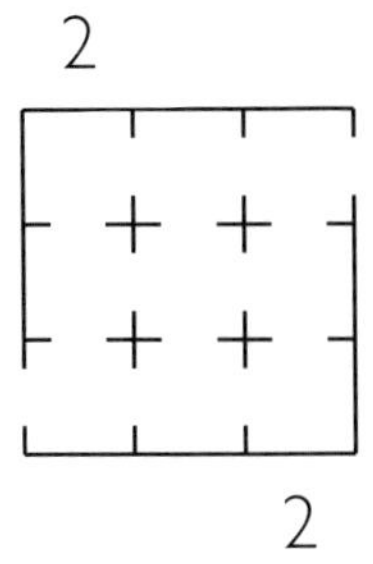

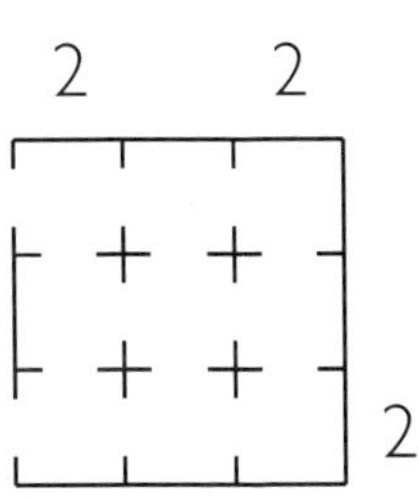

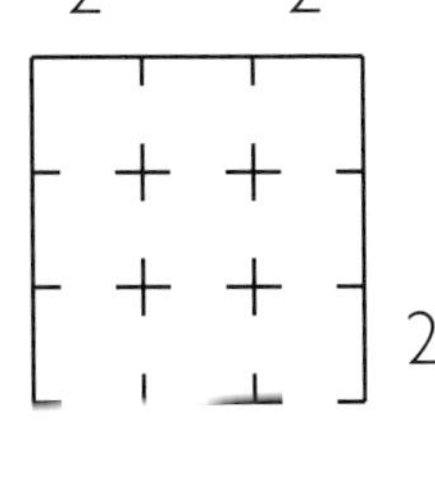

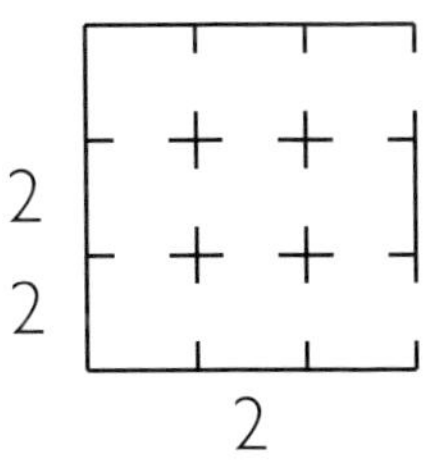

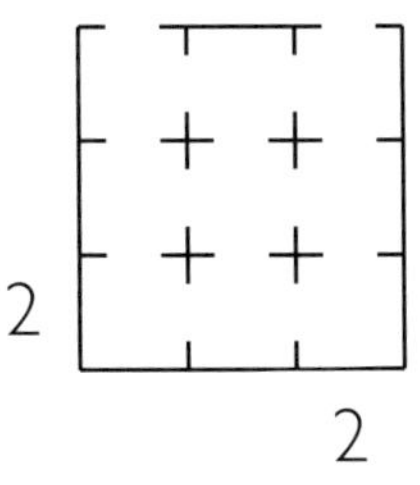

Solutions on page 89

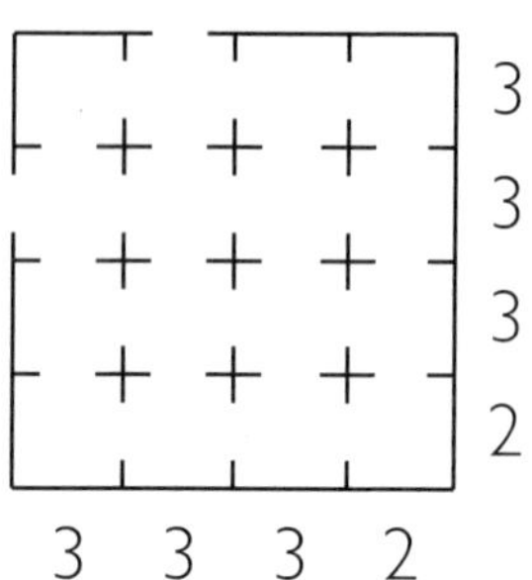

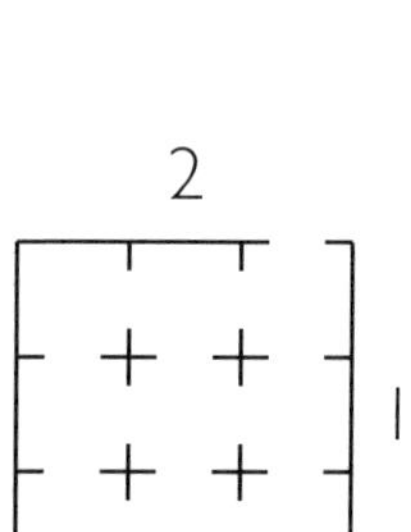

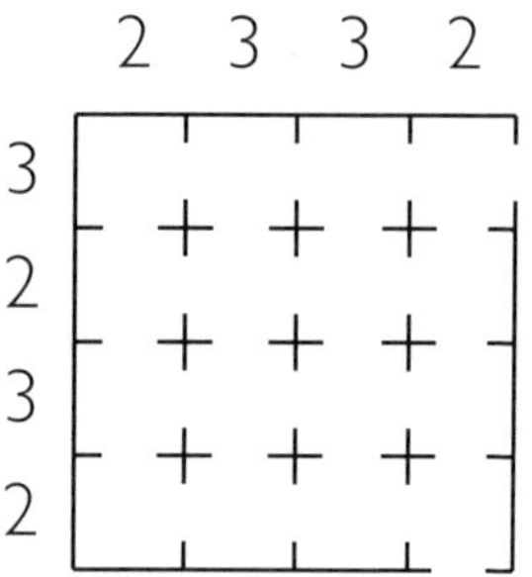

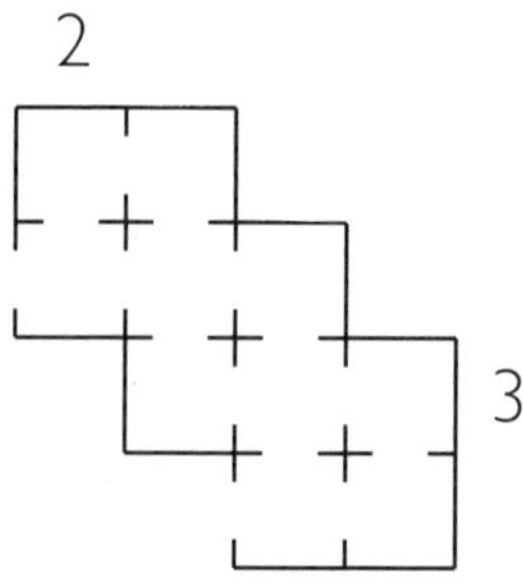

Solutions on page 90

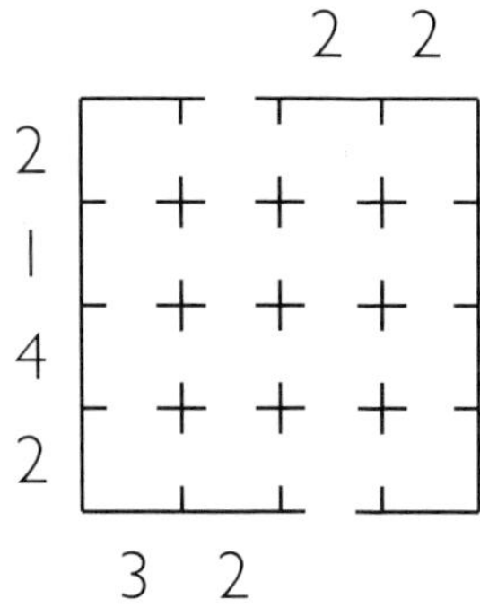

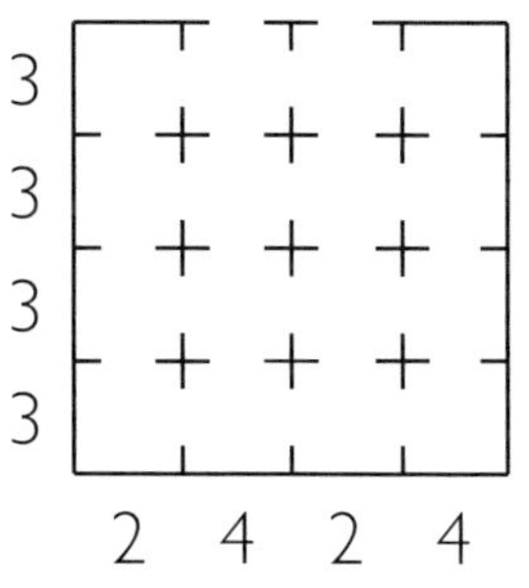

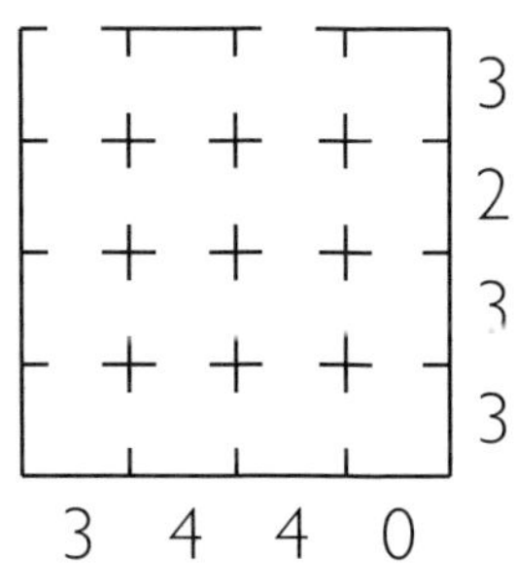

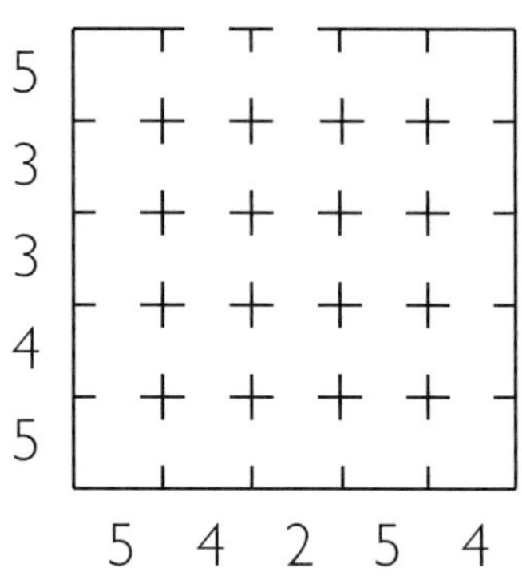

Solutions on page 90

If you don't know where you're going,
any path will take you there.

Lewis Carroll

Remember to keep an eye out for false entrances. Only the correct two entrances will work. Whenever a puzzle has false entrances, this symbol will alert you: ←?→

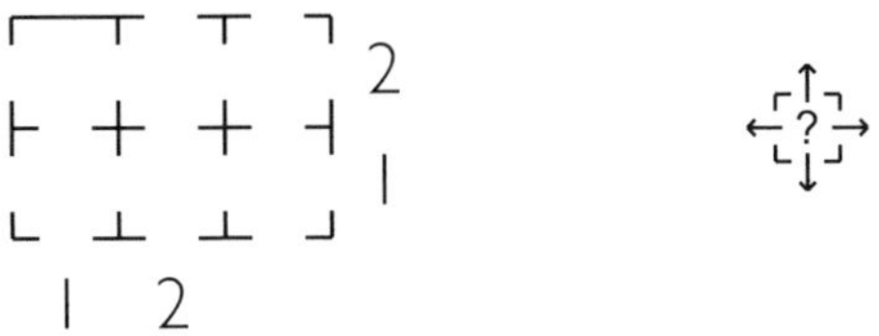

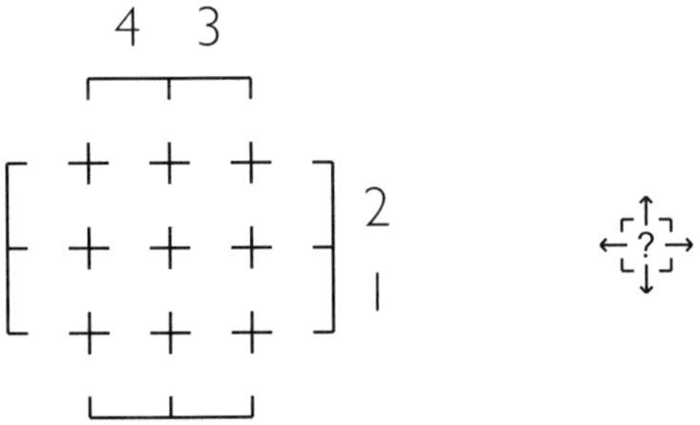

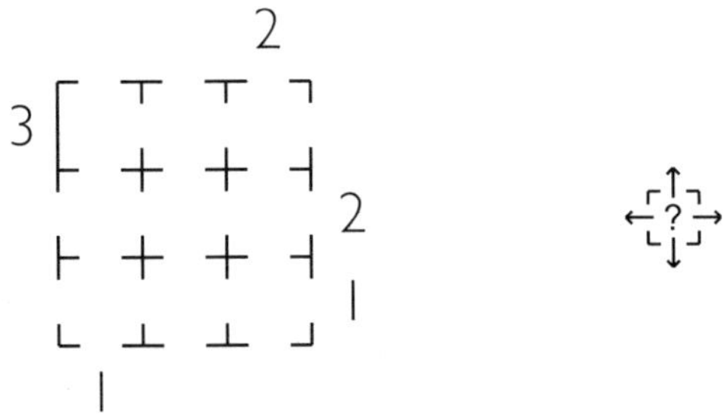

2
1
1 2

4 3
2
1

2
3
2
1
1

Solutions on page 90

0 0

0

2

2 4 3 1

1

2

3

4

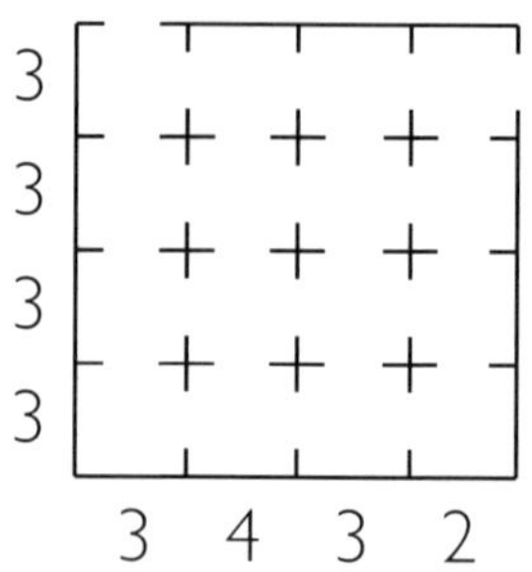

Solutions on page 90

2 3 4

1
2
3

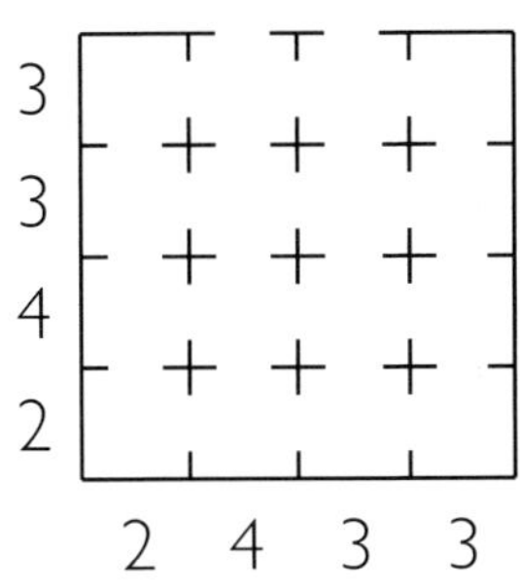

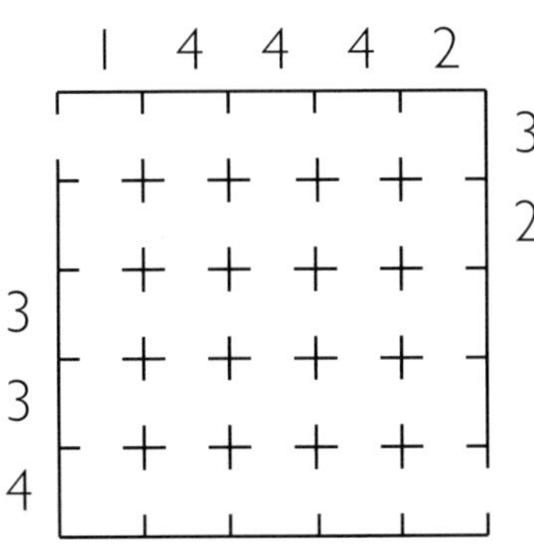

Solutions on page 91

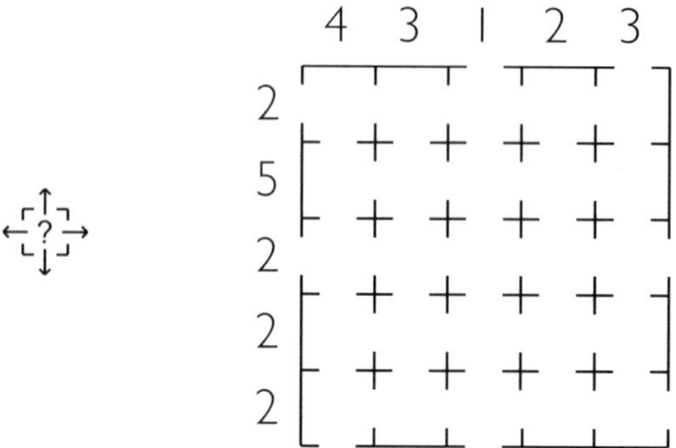

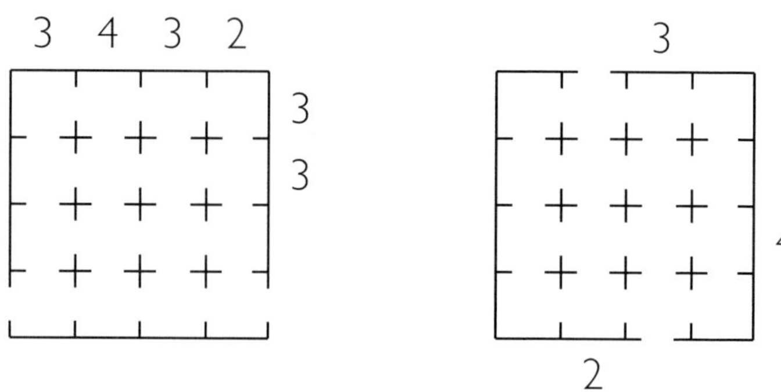

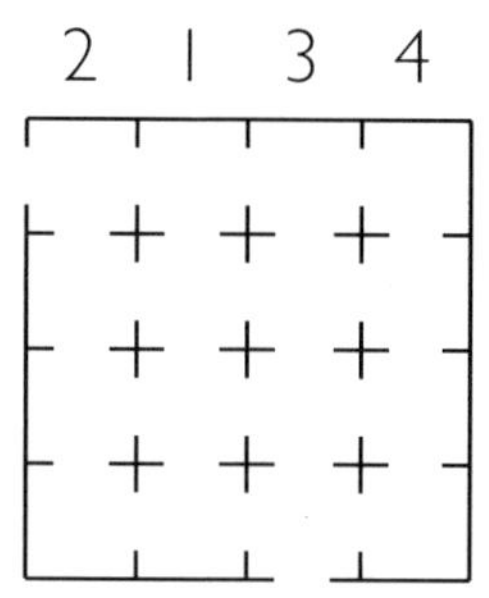

Solutions on page 91

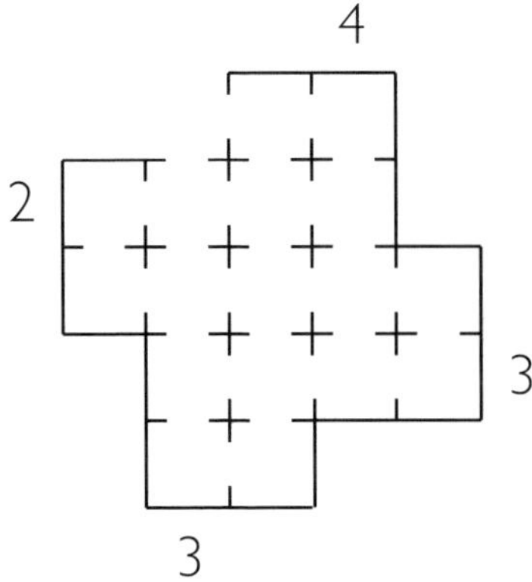

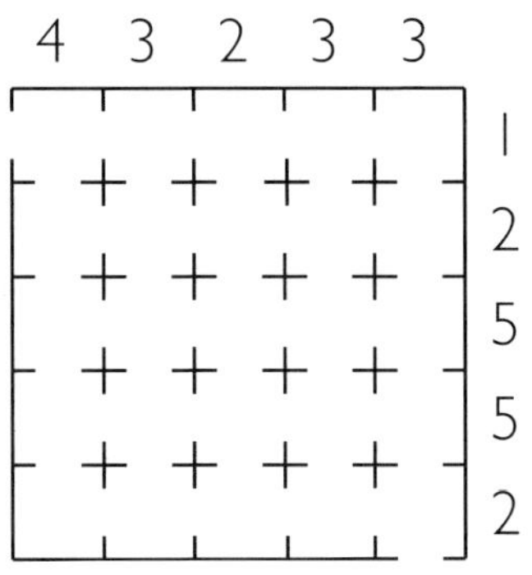

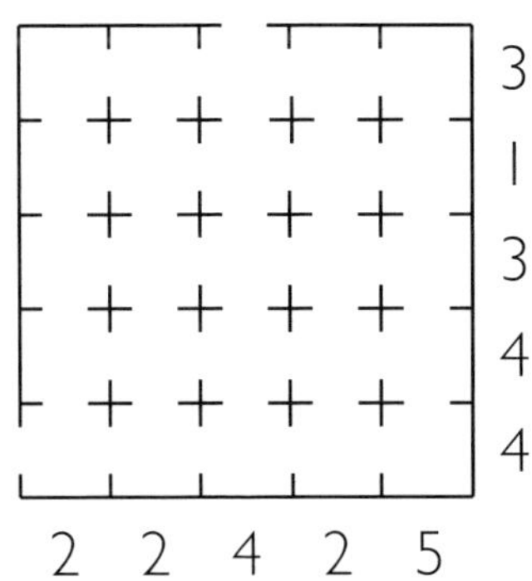

Solutions on page 91

A blocked path also offers guidance.

Mason Cooley

Now you will begin to see numbers adjacent to more than one row or column. For help with interpreting these, see the special instructions on page 12.

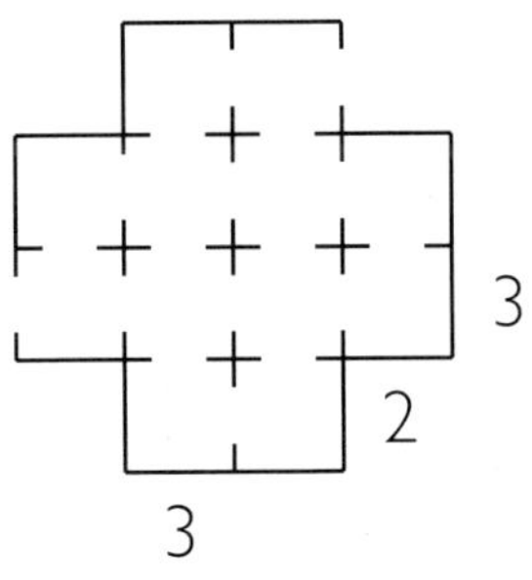

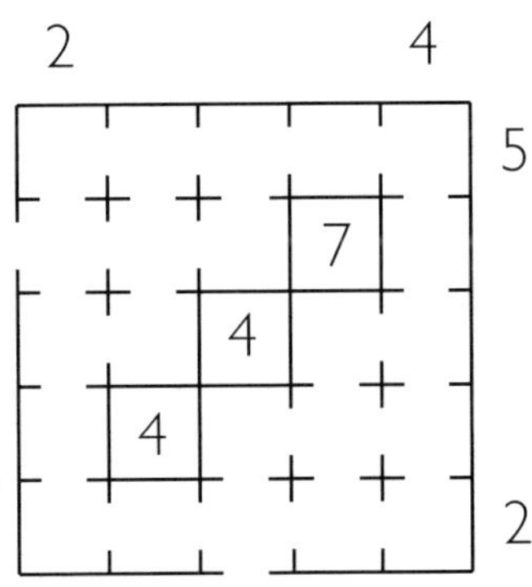

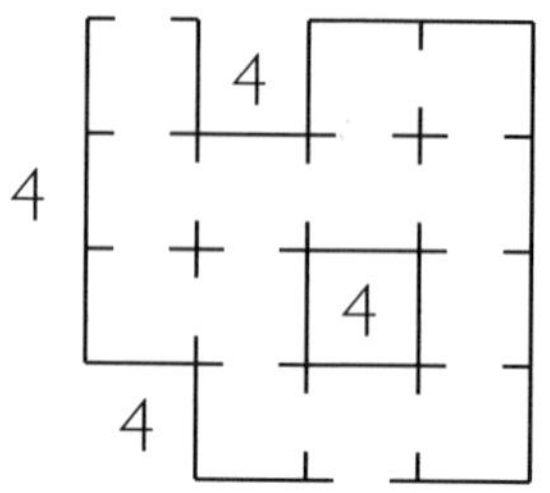

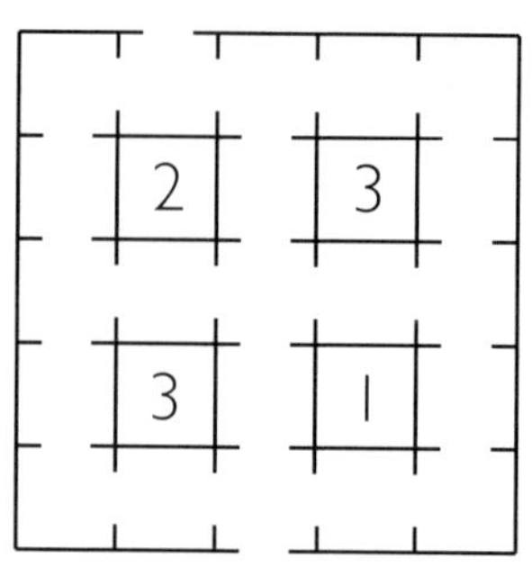

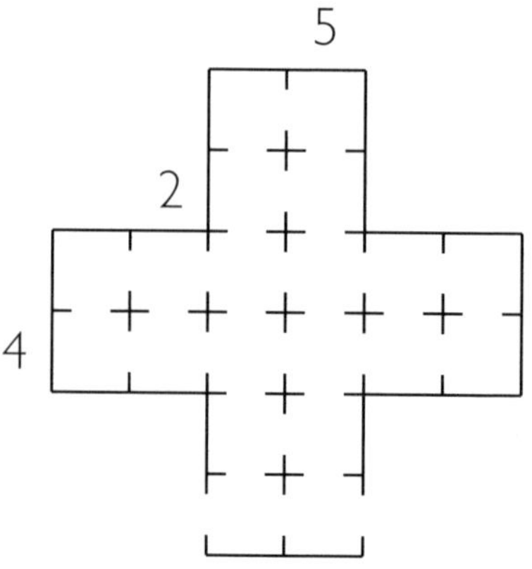

Solutions on page 92

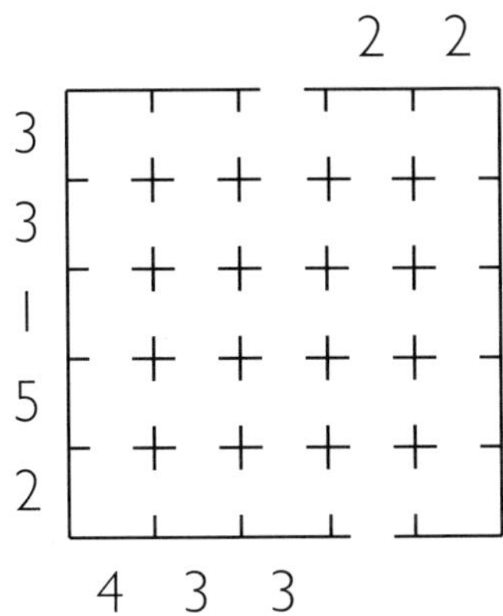

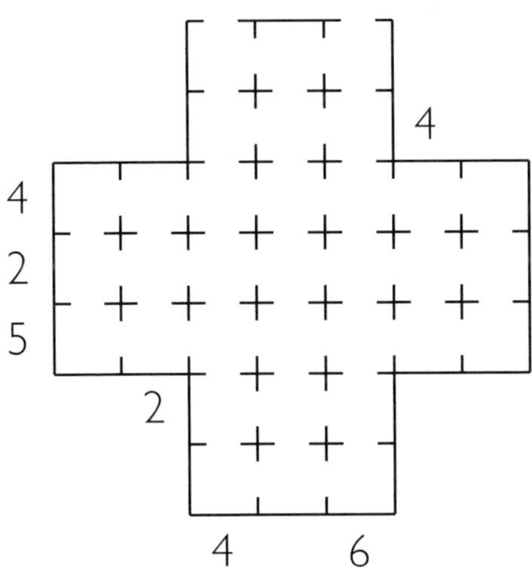

Solutions on page 92

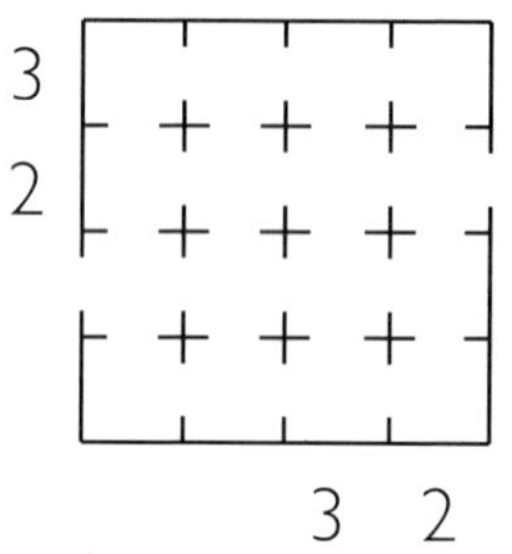

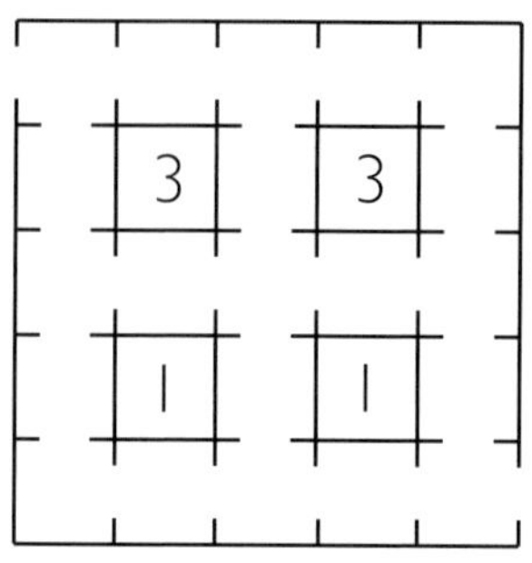

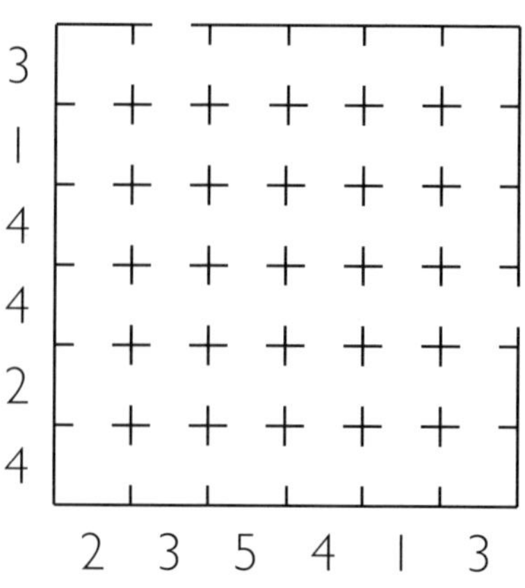

Solutions on page 92

	6	7			
					2
					3
					2
					1
					4
2					
2					
3					
2					
4					
			5	7	

4 3

2 1

Solutions on page 92

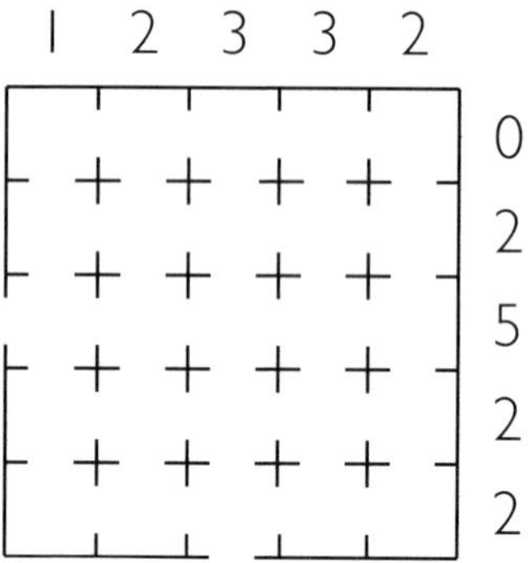

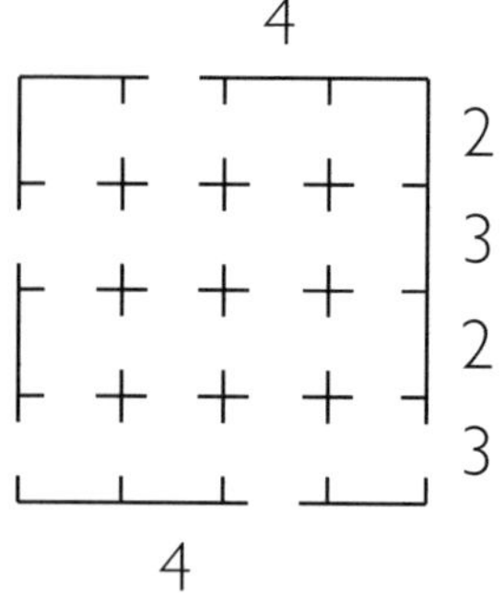

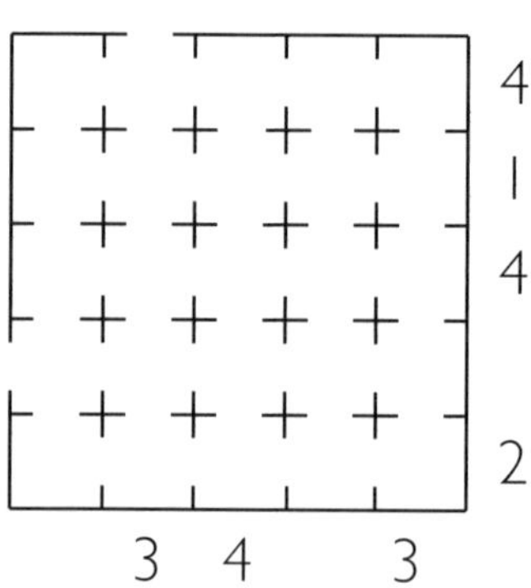

Solutions on page 93

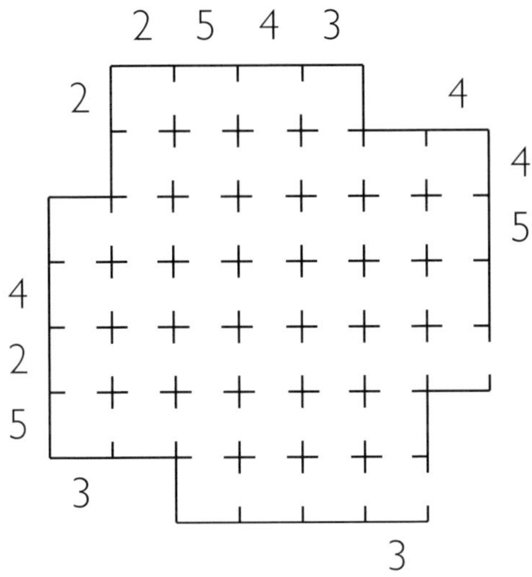

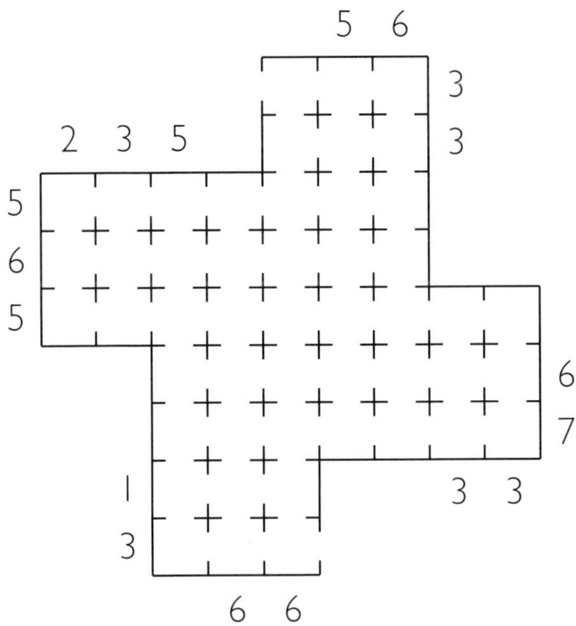

Solutions on page 93

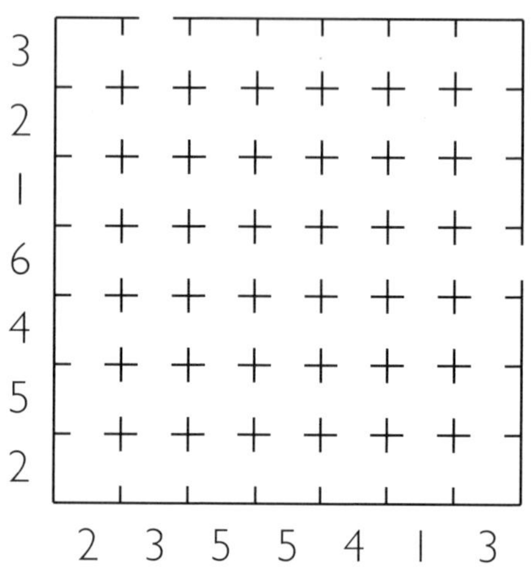

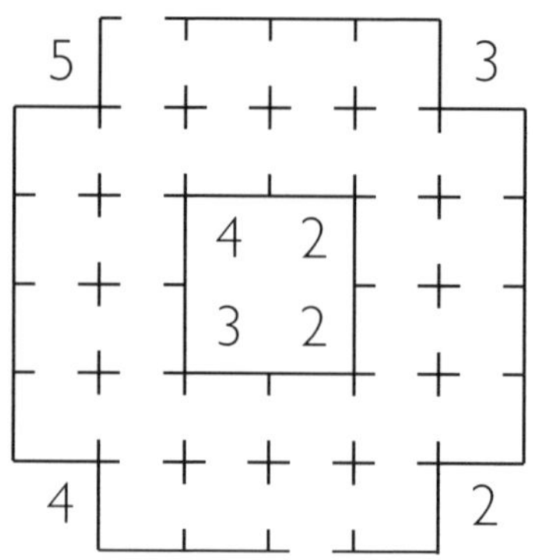

Solutions on page 93

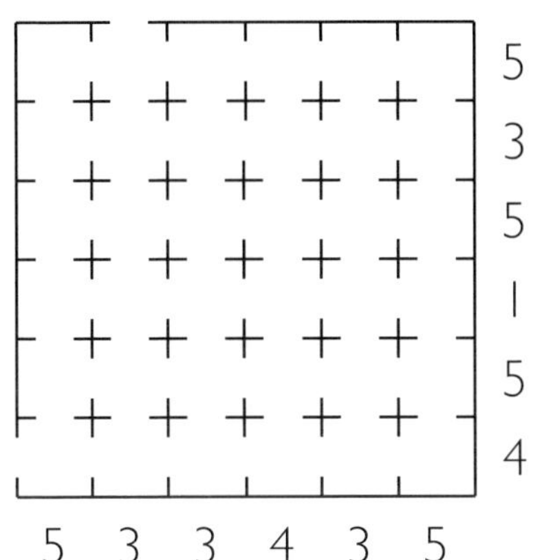

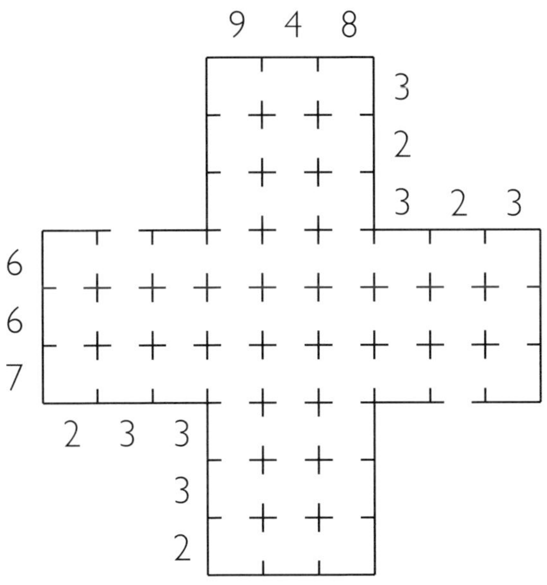

Solutions on page 93

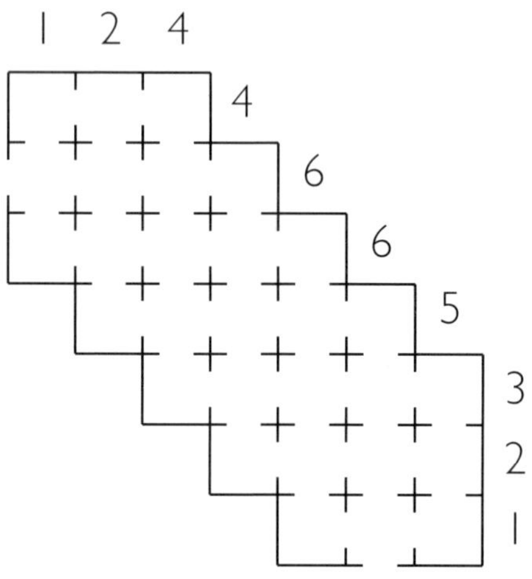

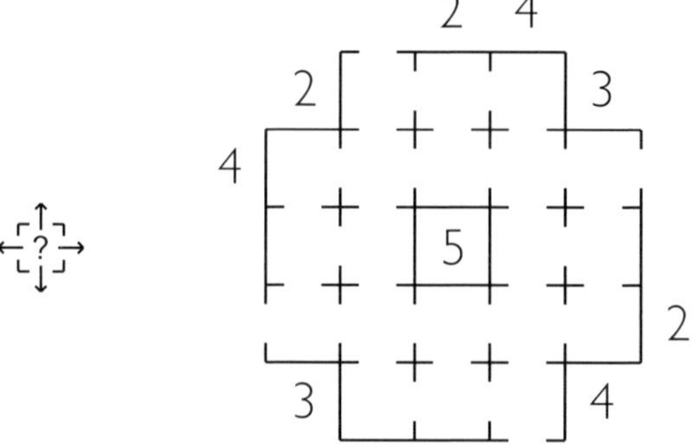

Solutions on page 94

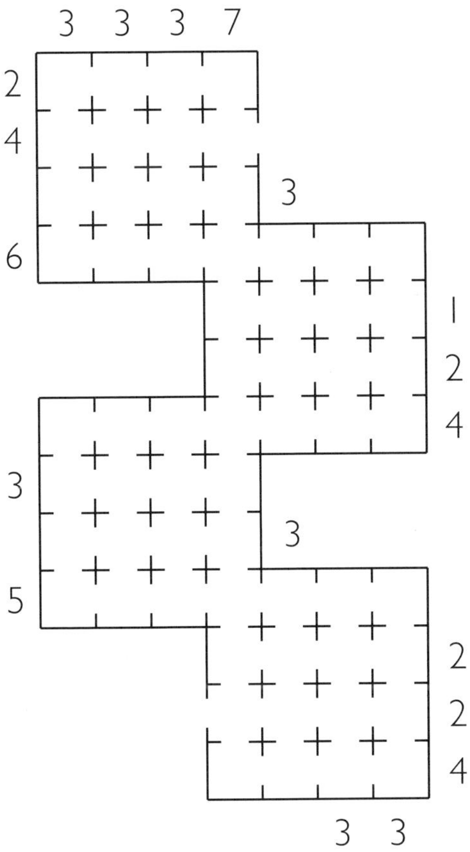

Solution on page 94

In the middle of the journey of our life I came to myself within a dark wood where the straight way was lost.

Dante Alighieri

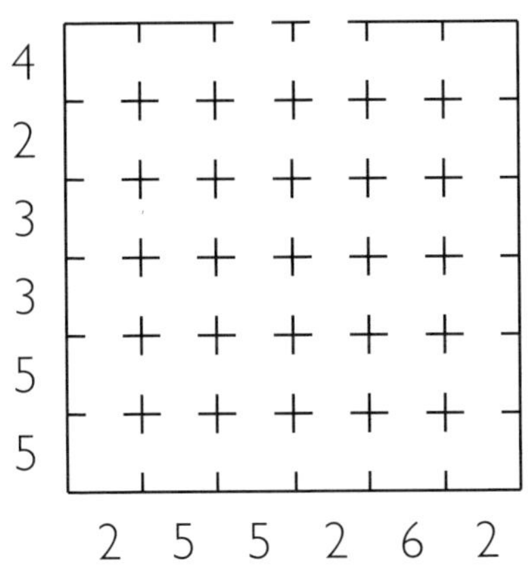

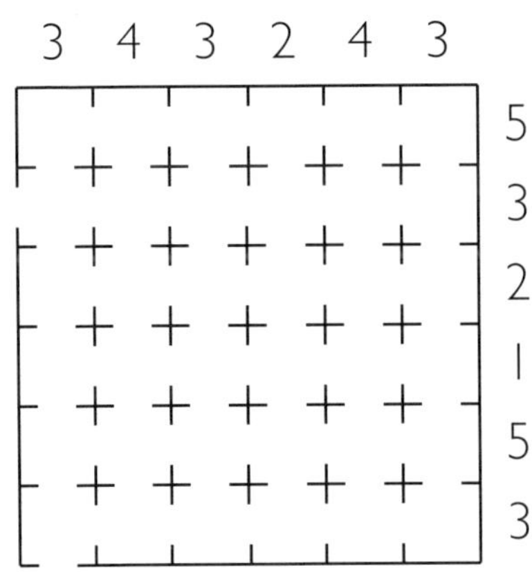

Solutions on page 94

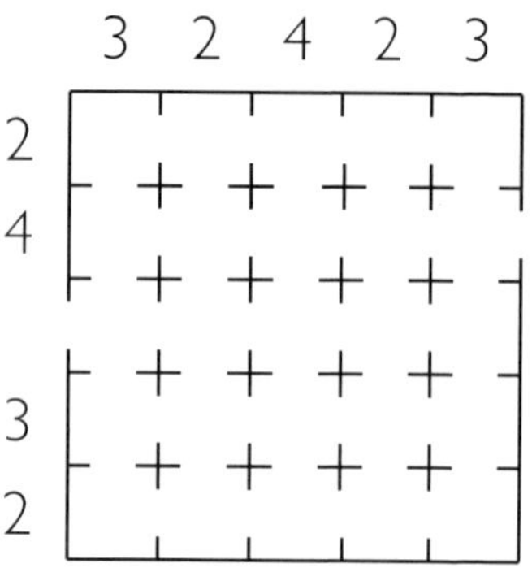

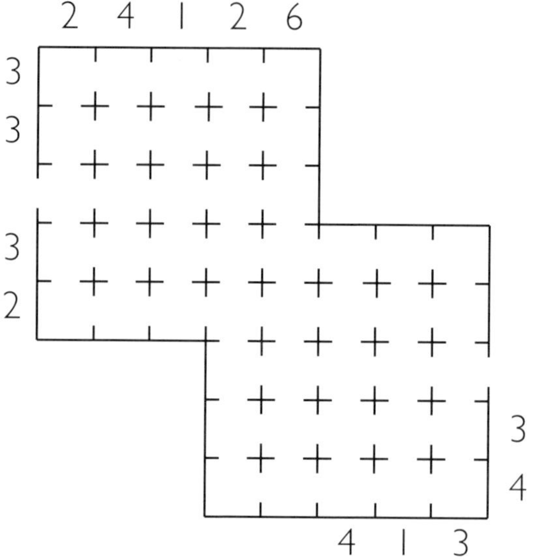

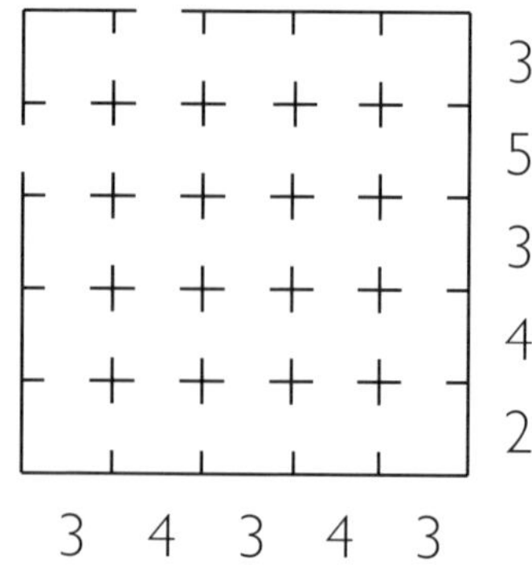

Solutions on page 94

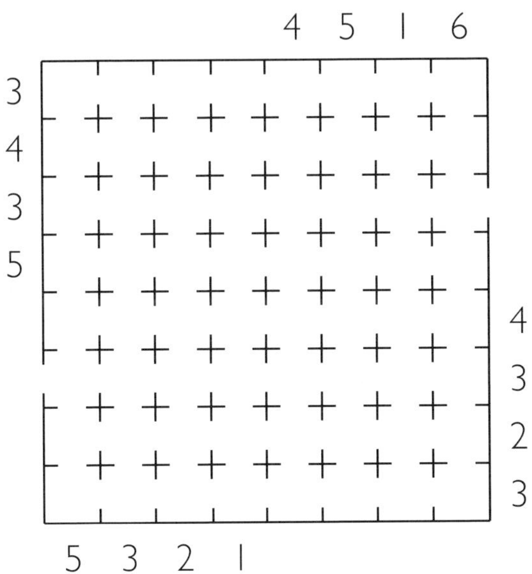

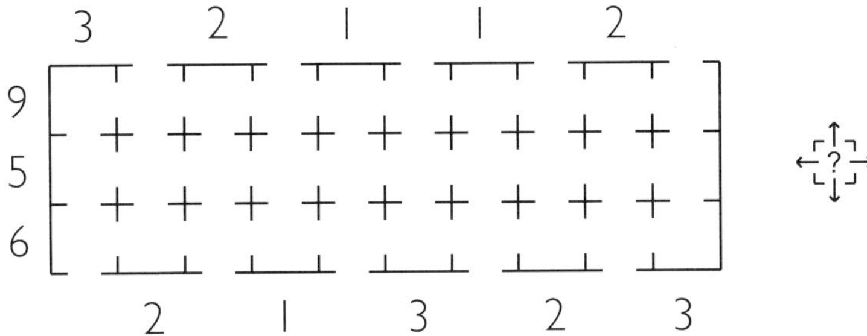

Solutions on page 95

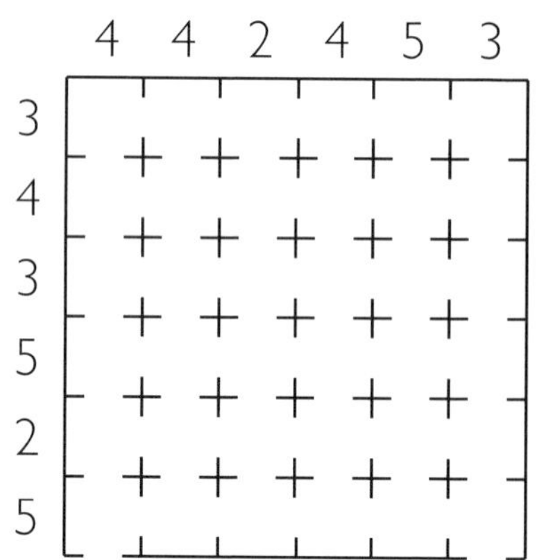

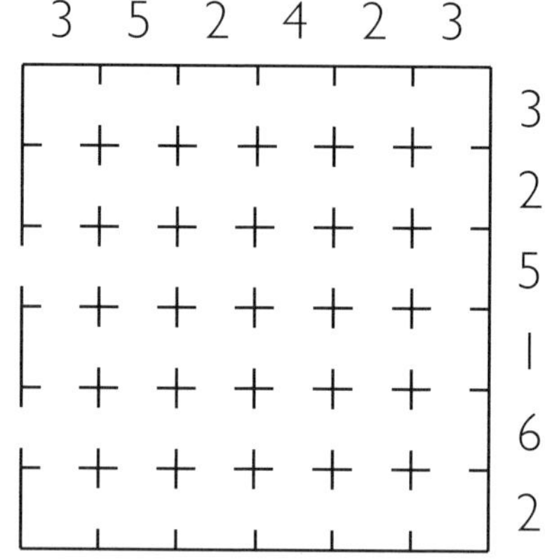

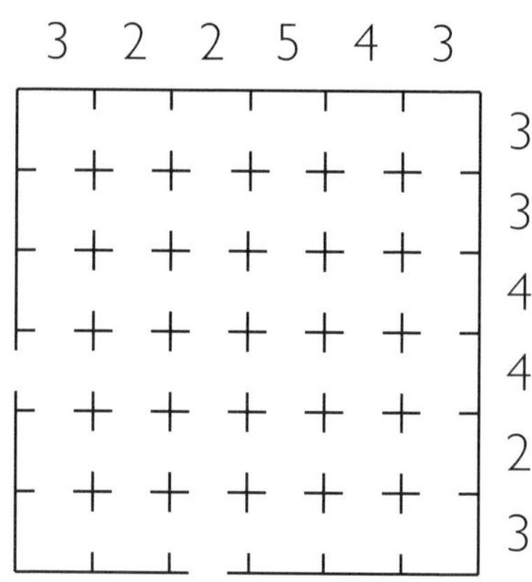

Solutions on page 95

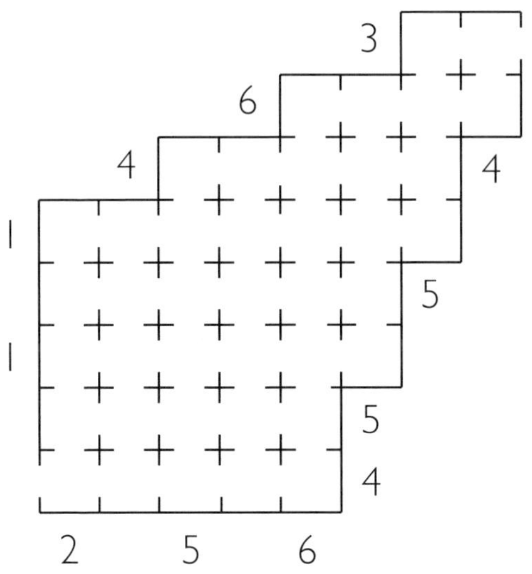

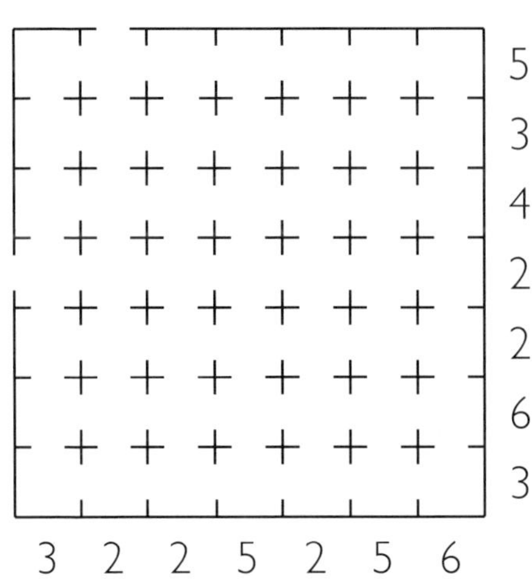

Solutions on page 95

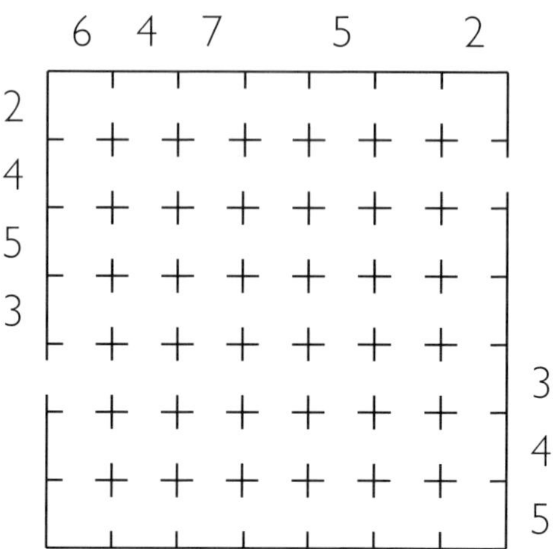

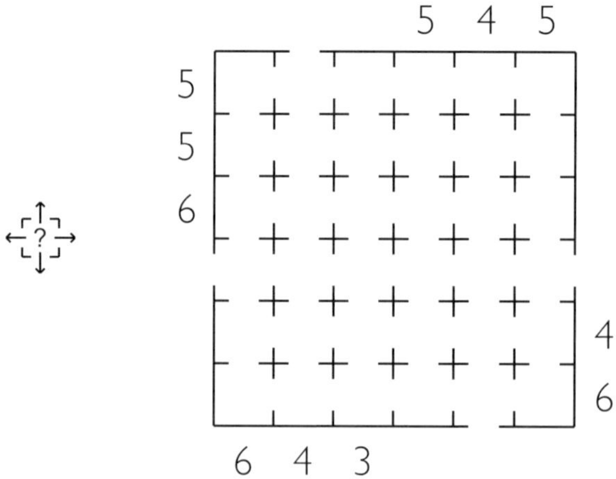

Solutions on page 95

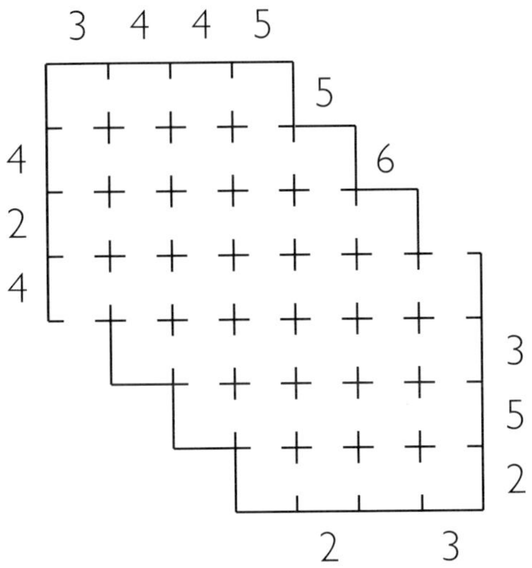

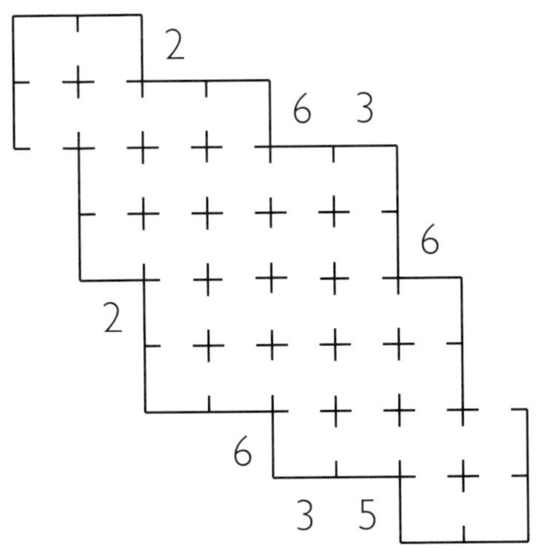

Solutions on page 96

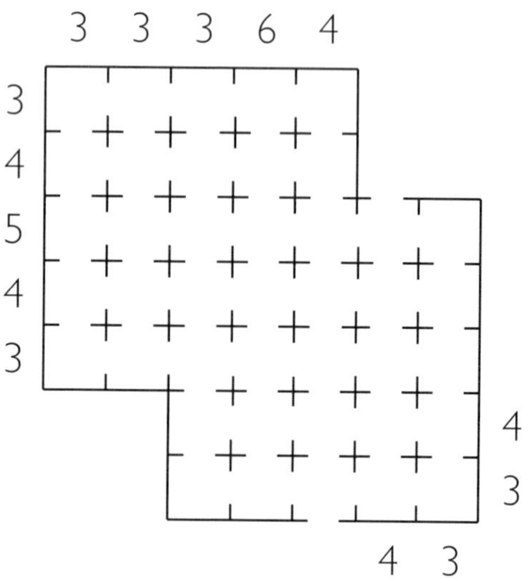

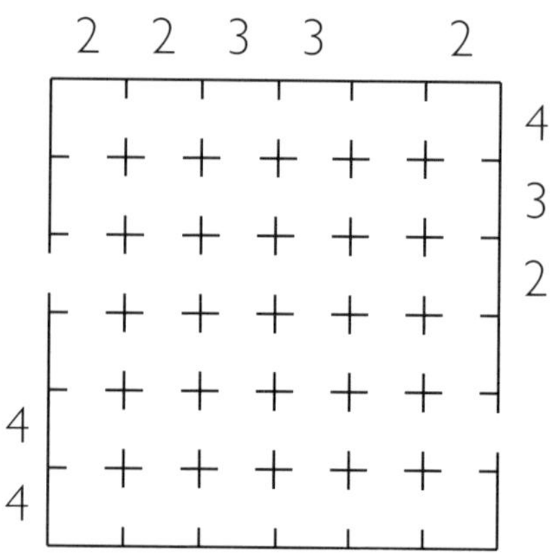

Solutions on page 96

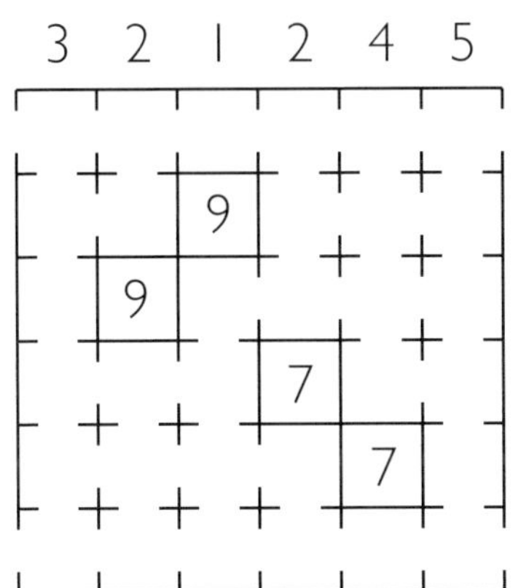

4 4 2

3

2

4 1

2 1

1

4

Solutions on page 96

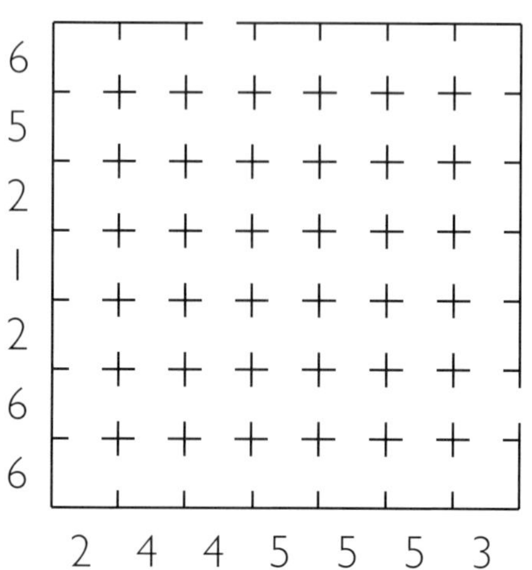

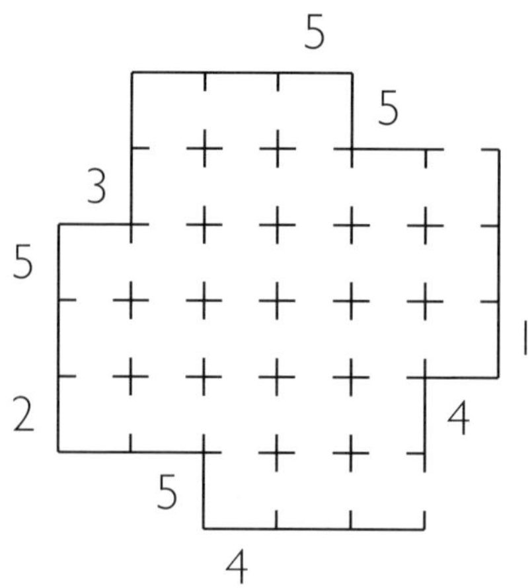

Solutions on page 96

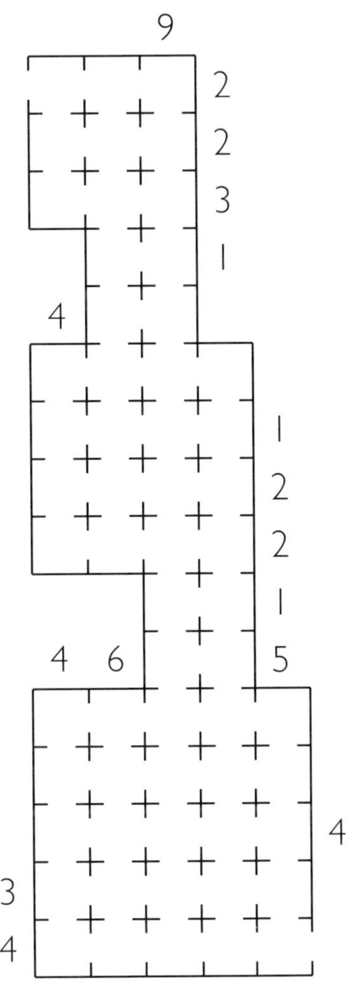

Solution on page 97

All paths are the same, leading nowhere. Therefore, pick a path with heart!

Carlos Castaneda

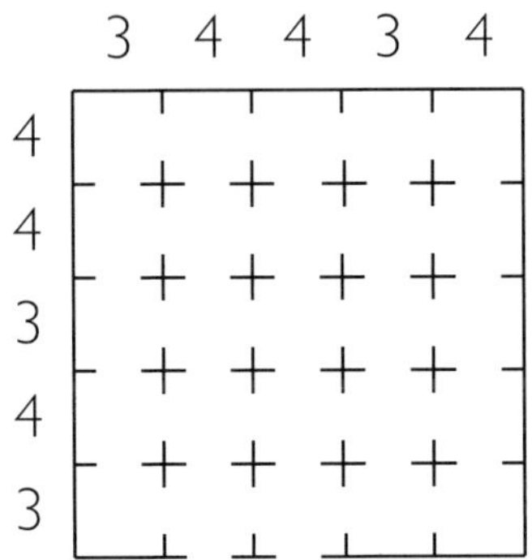

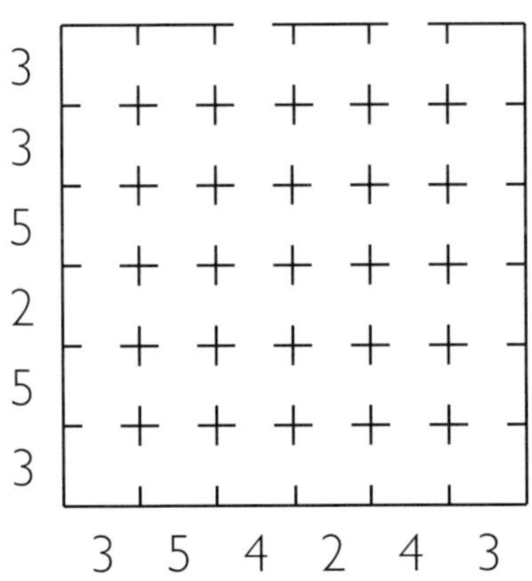

Solutions on page 97

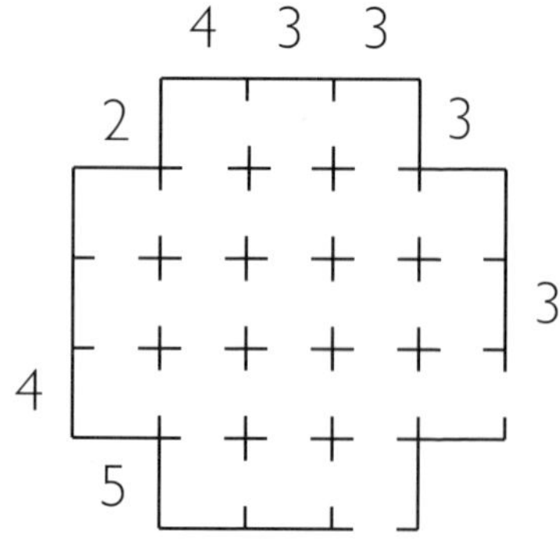

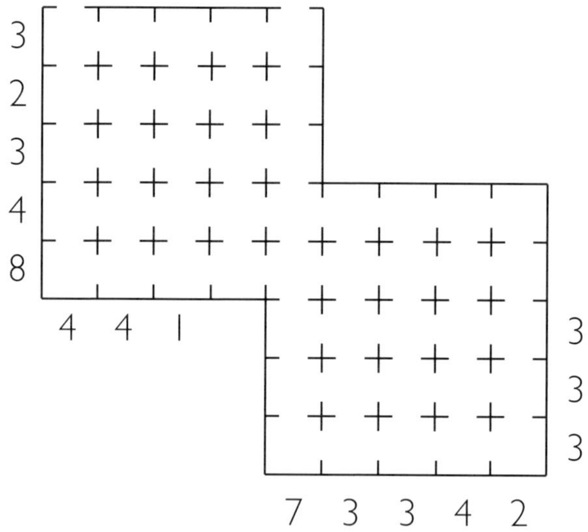

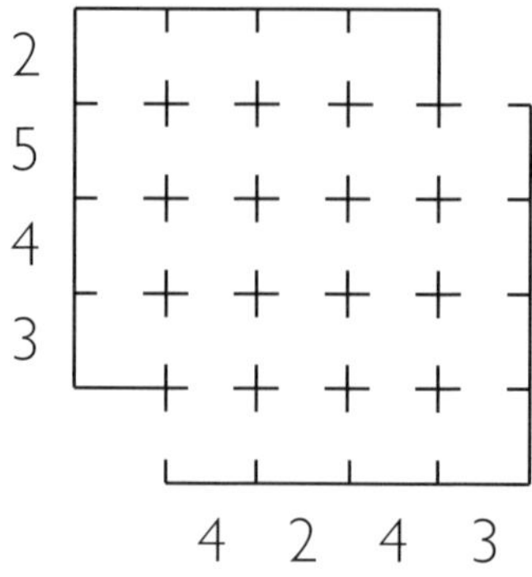

Solutions on page 97

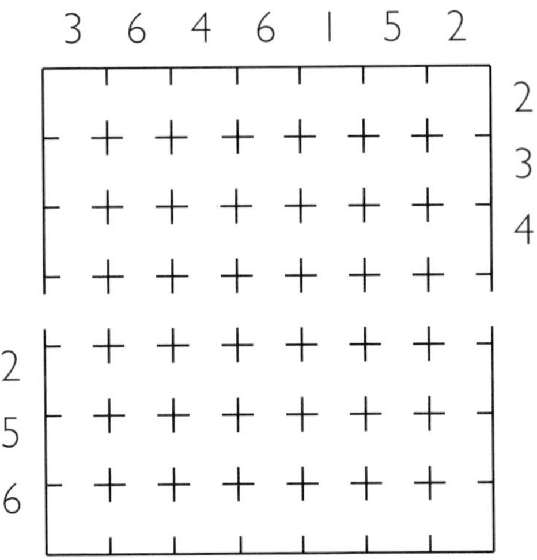

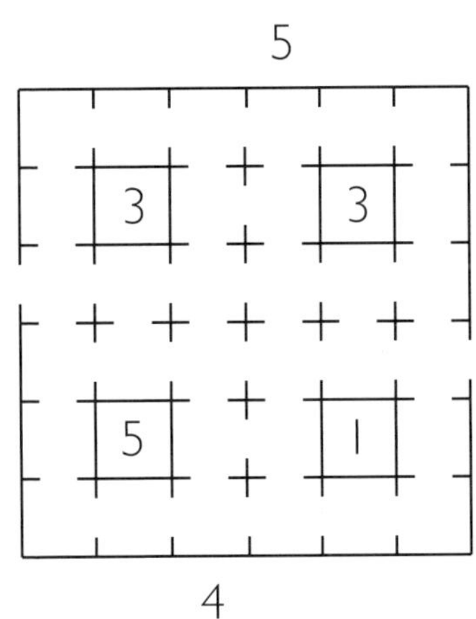

Solutions on page 97

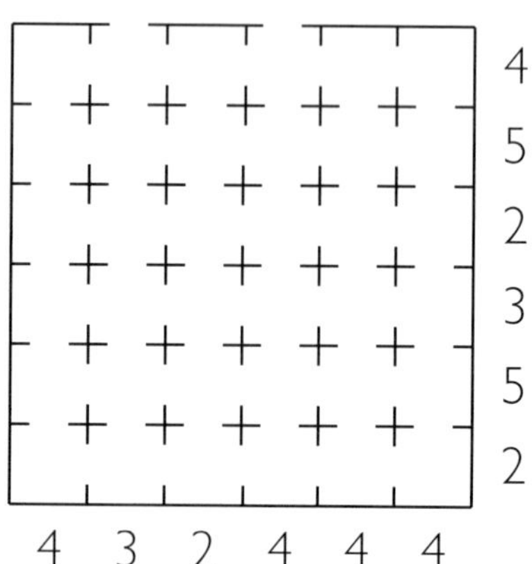

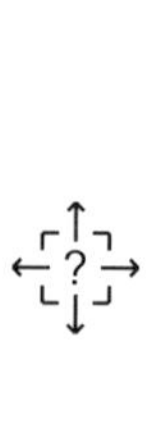

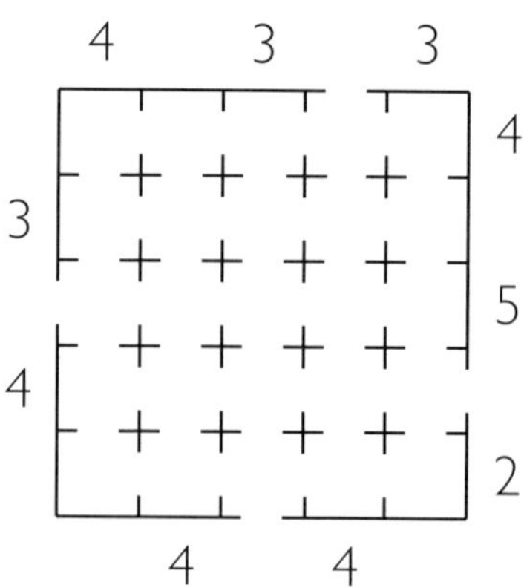

Solutions on page 98

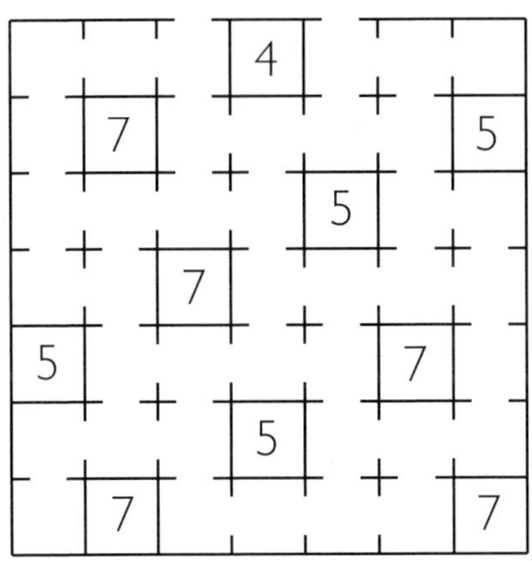

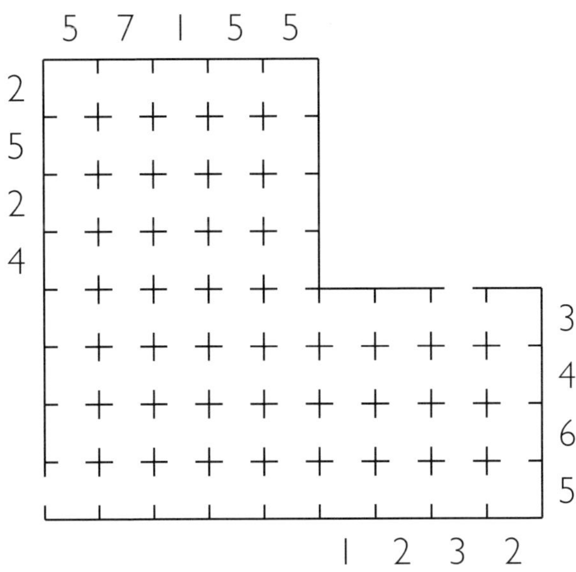

Solutions on page 98

6

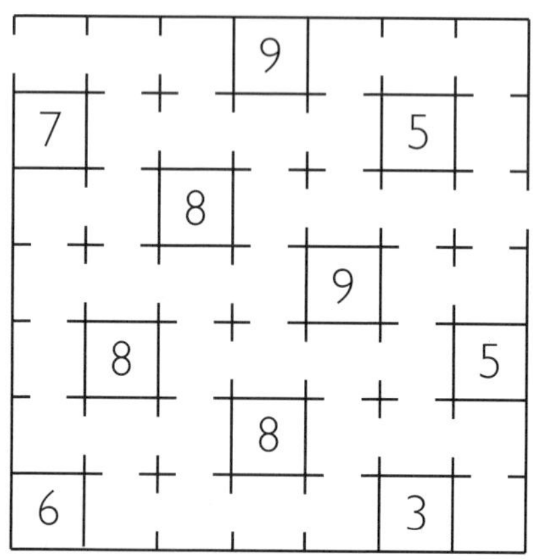

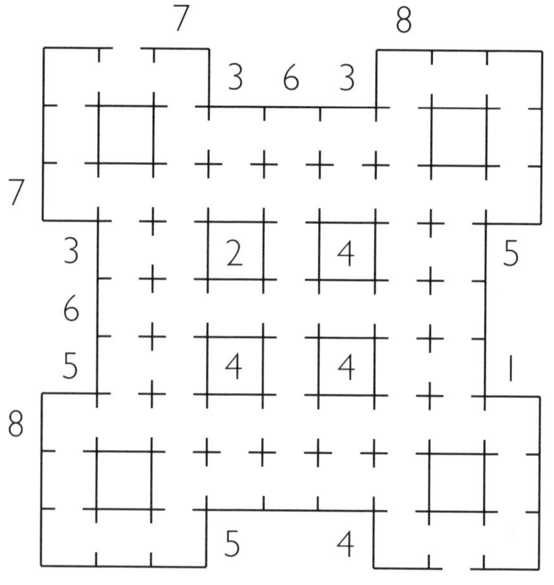

Solutions on page 98

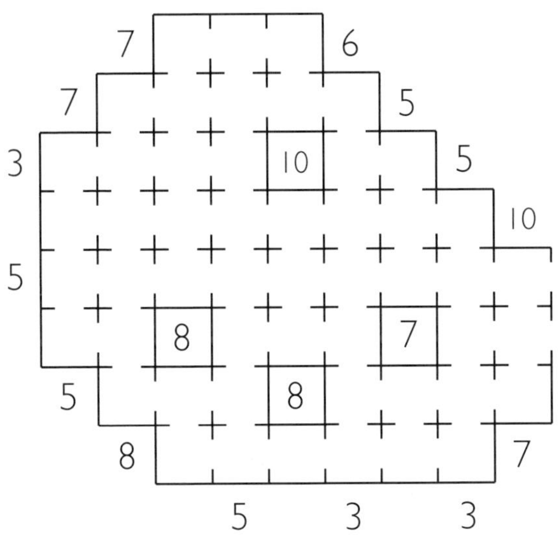

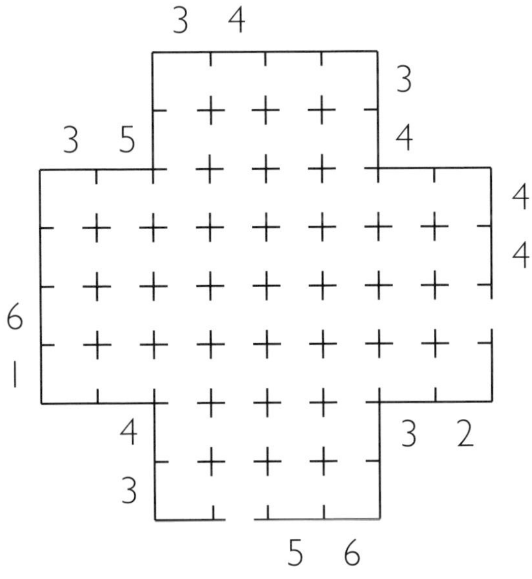

Solutions on page 98

If you find a path with no obstacles, it probably doesn't lead anywhere.

Frank Howard Clark

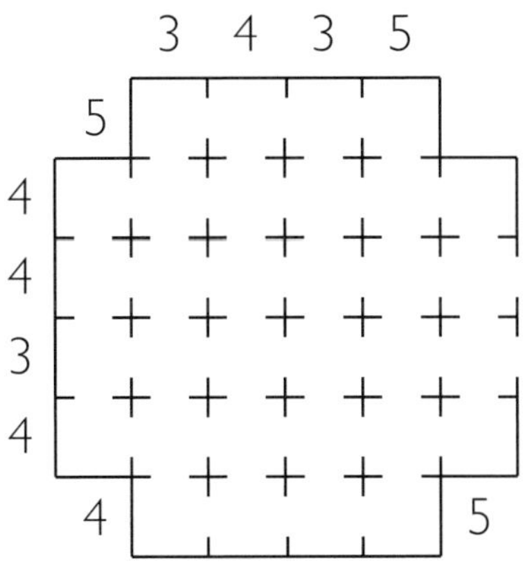

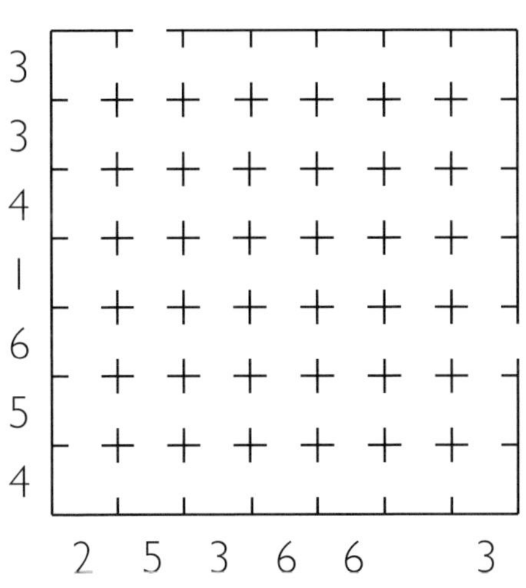

Solutions on page 99

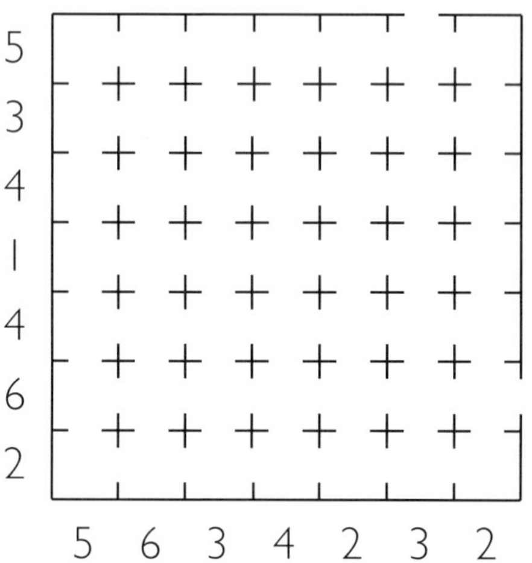

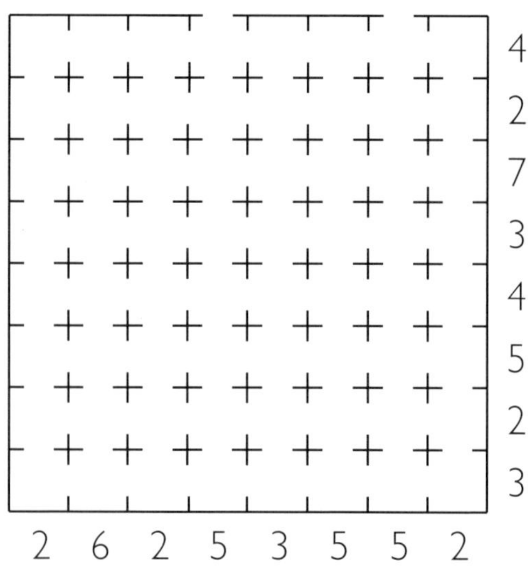

 Solutions on page 99

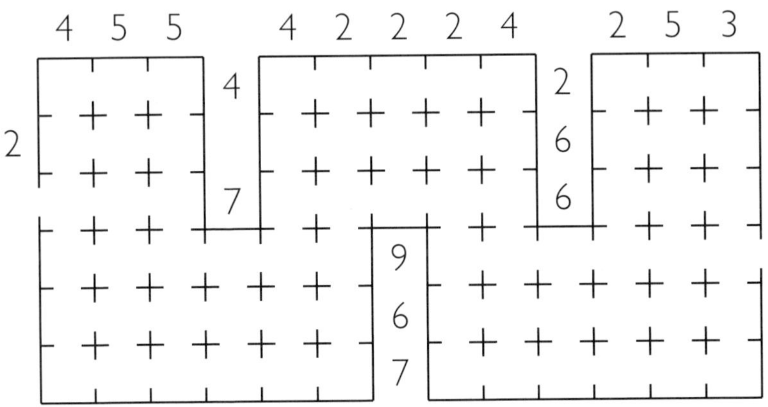

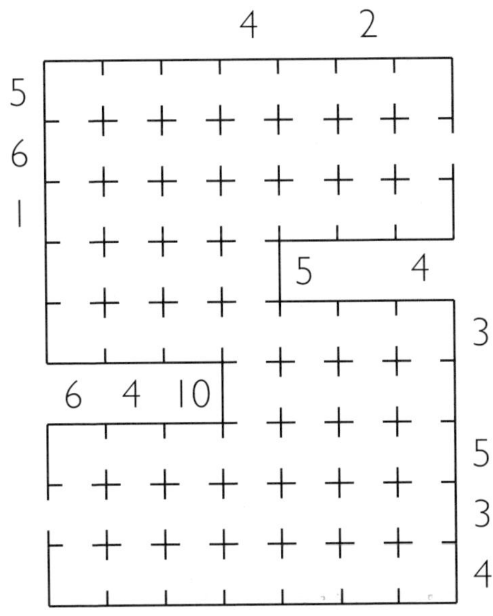

Solutions on page 99

7

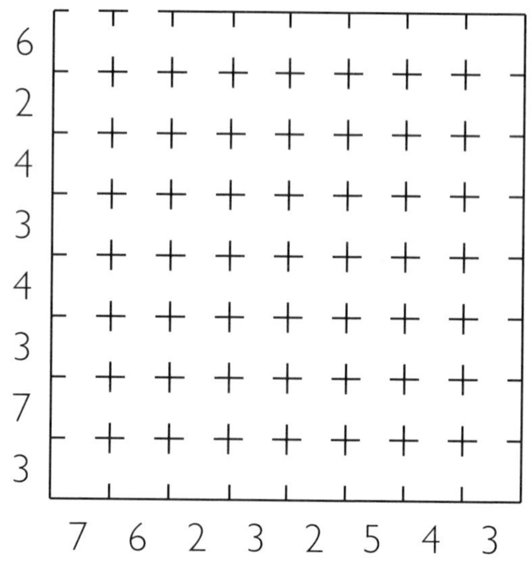

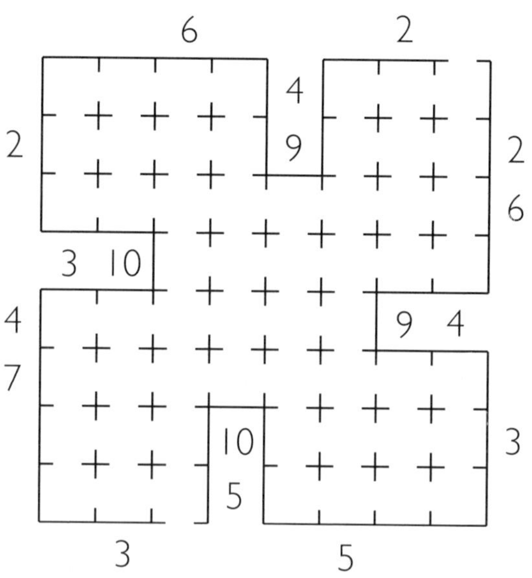

Solutions on page 99

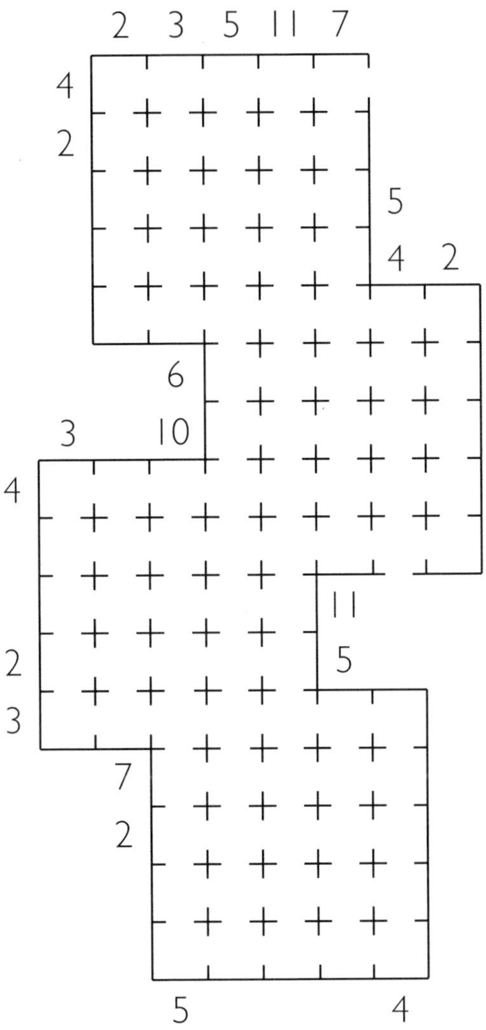

Solution on page 100

7

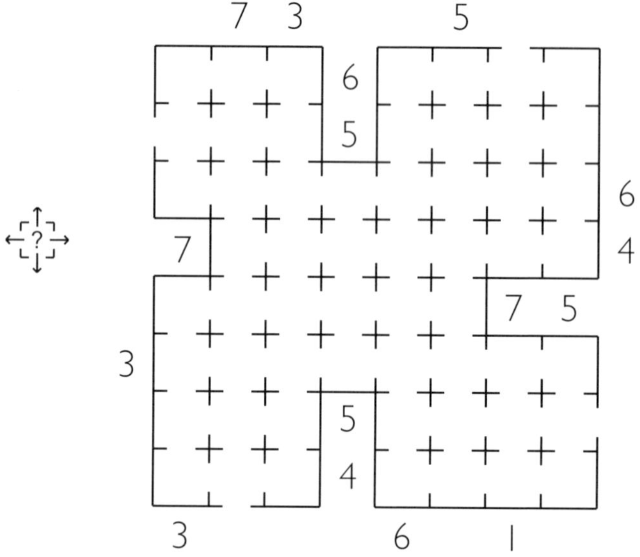

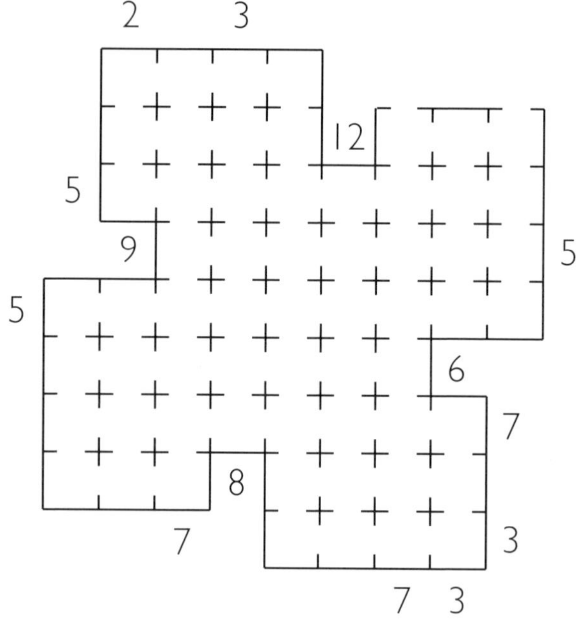

 Solutions on page 100

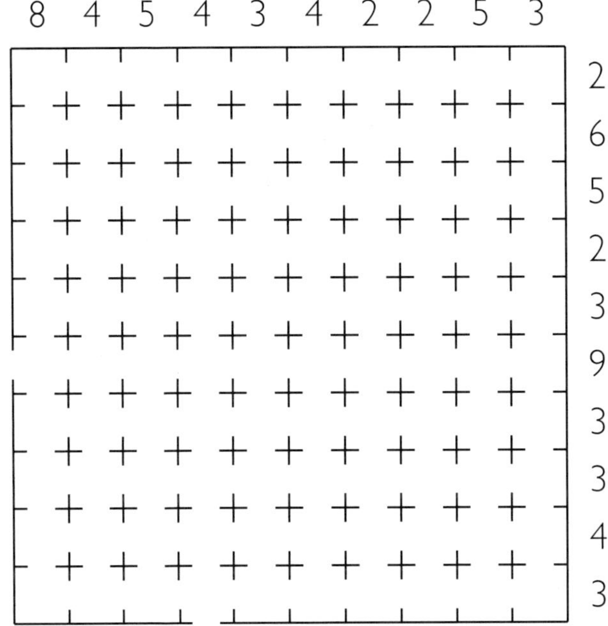

Solution on page 100

7

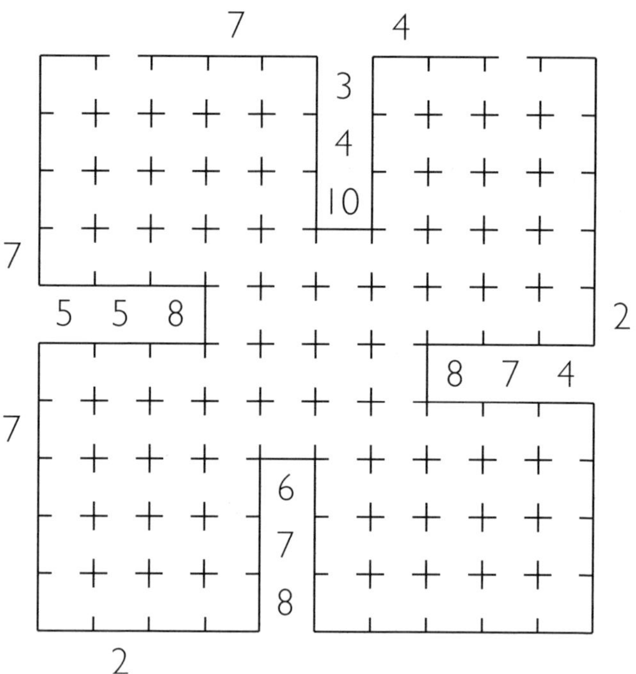

Solution on page 100

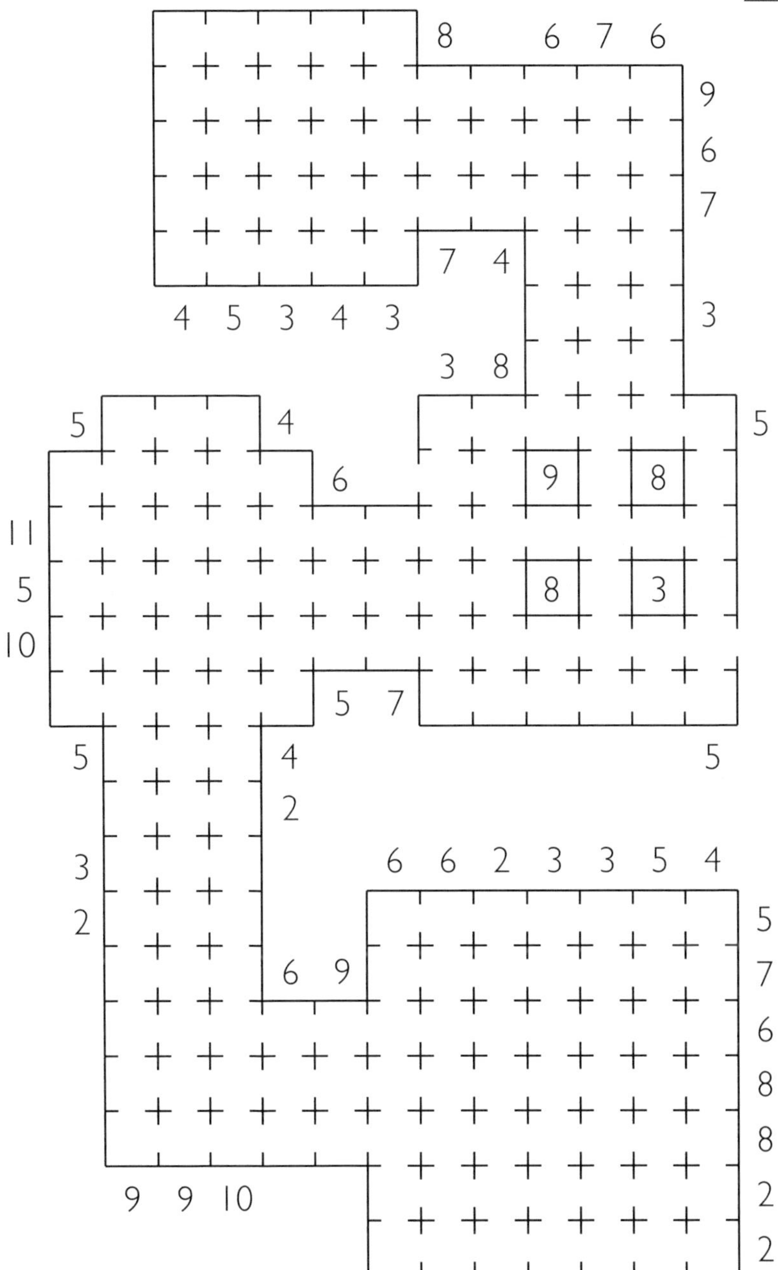

Solution on page 101

A good puzzle, it's a fair thing. Nobody is lying. It's very clear, and the problem depends just on you.

Erno Rubik

Encrypted Path Puzzles

In this section, the puzzles are just like the others in the book with one difference. The numbers are encrypted. For each puzzle, a unique code has been devised so the numbers are each represented by a letter. The encryption is one-to-one. This means that all instances of a given number are represented by the same letter and all instances of a given letter represent the same number.

A puzzle that would previously have looked like this...

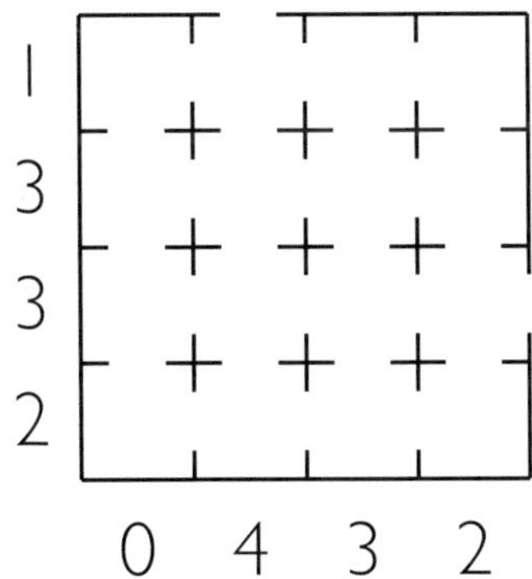

...will now look like this.

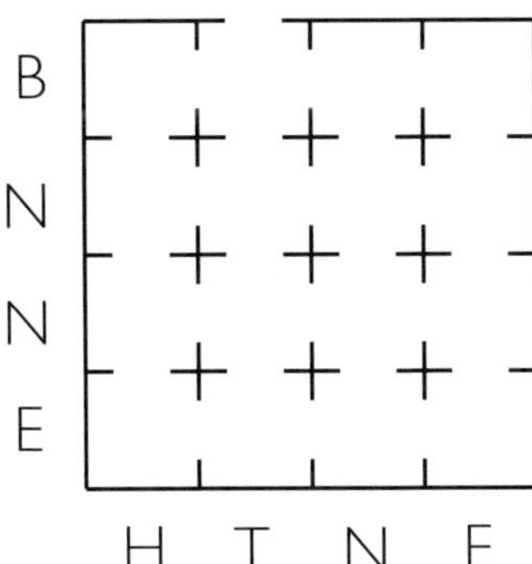

Have fun!

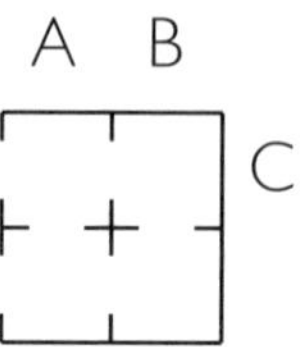

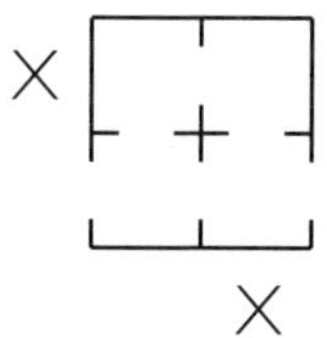

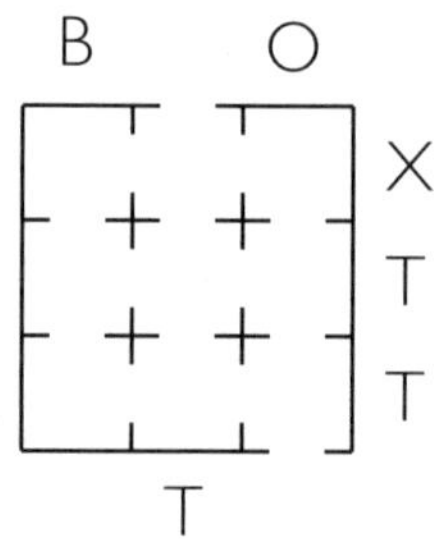

Solutions on page 101

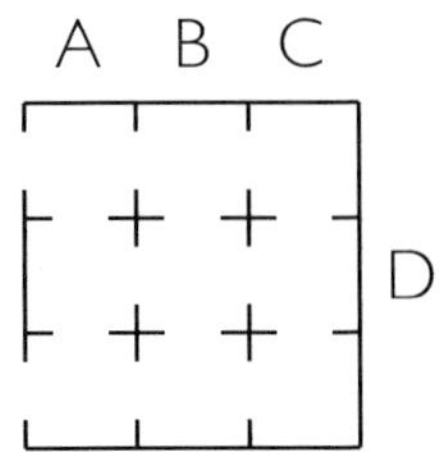

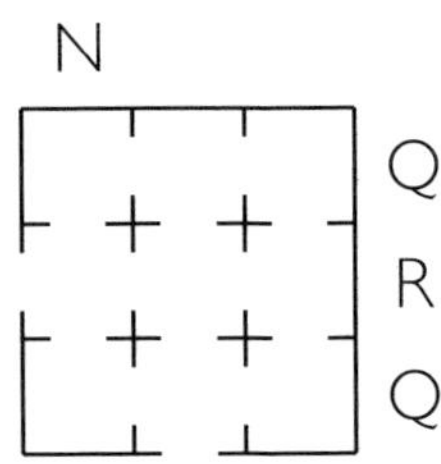

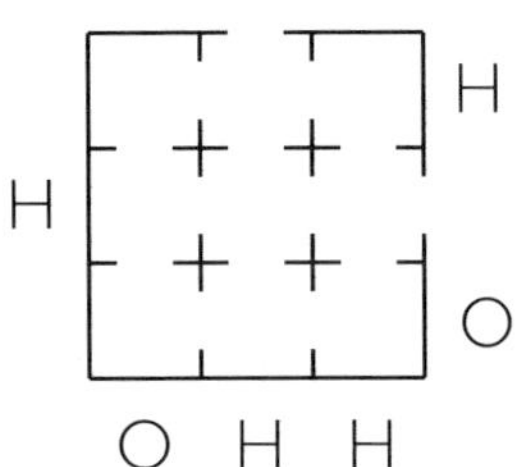

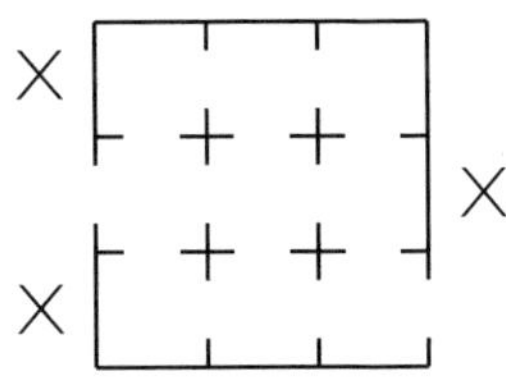

Solutions on page 101

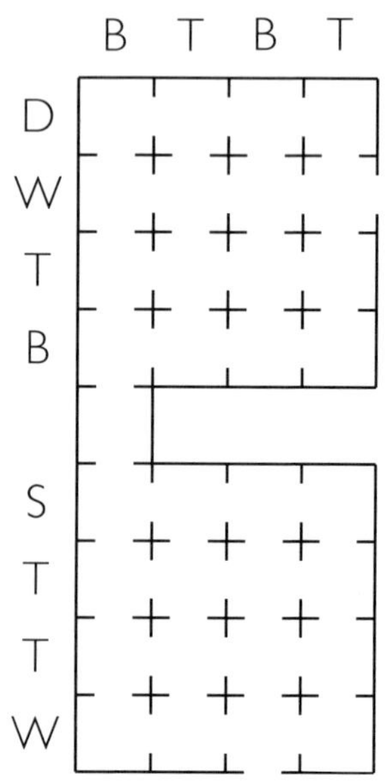

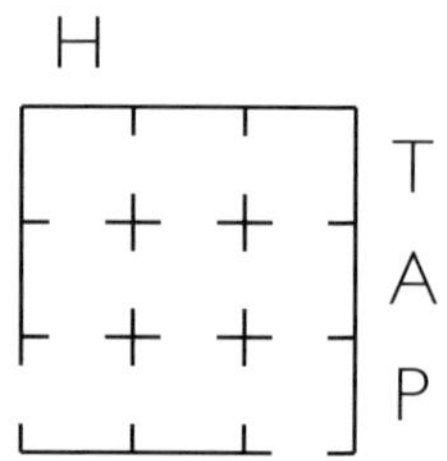

Solutions on page 101

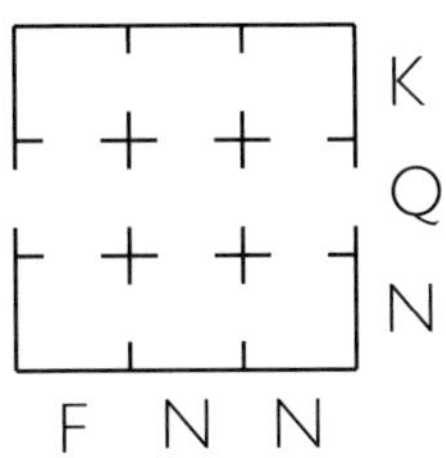

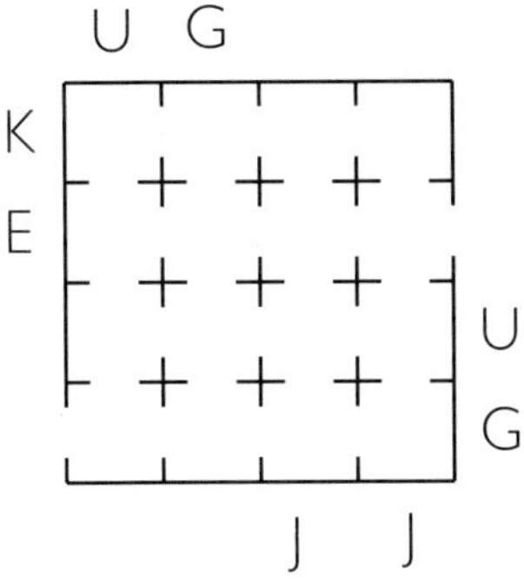

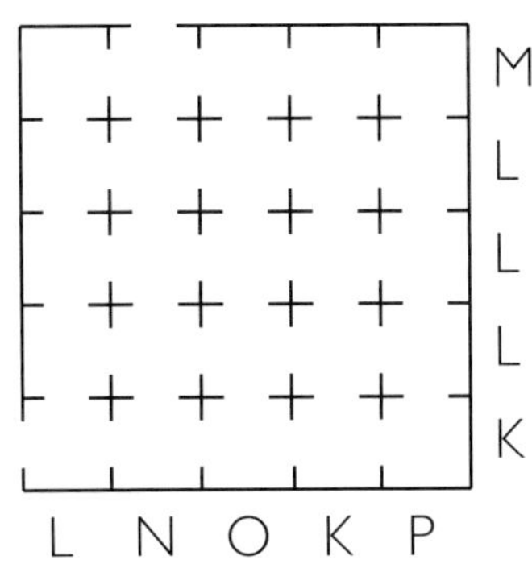

Solutions on page 102

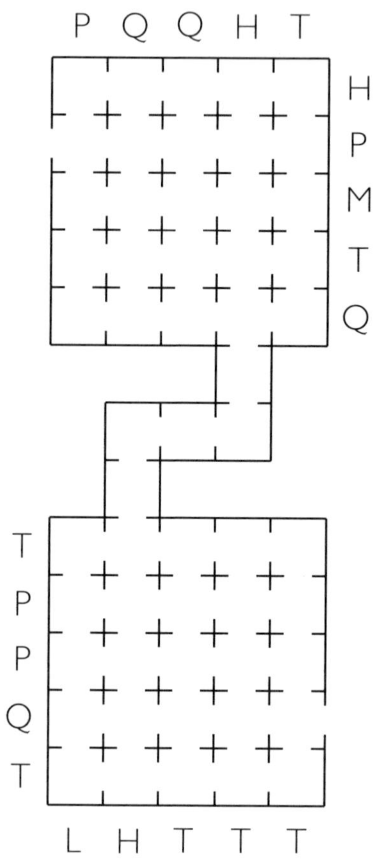

Solutions on page 102

The truth is of course is that
there is no journey.
We are arriving and departing all
at the same time.

David Bowie

Solutions are not the answer.

Richard M. Nixon

Solutions

LEVEL: 1

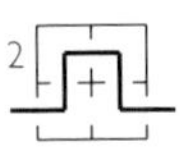

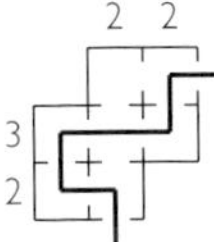

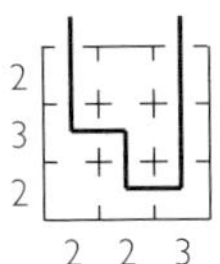

Page 25

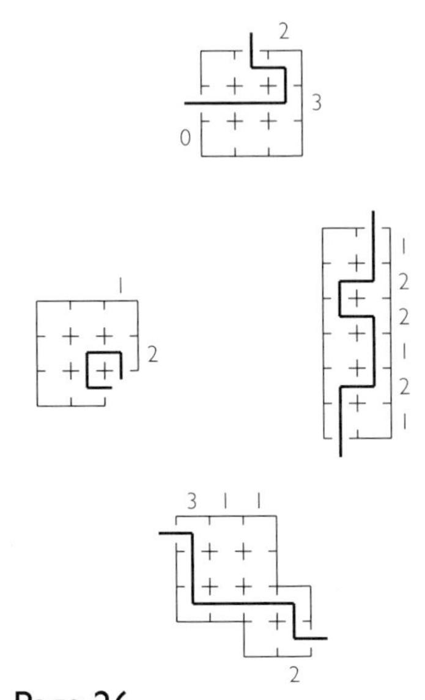

Page 26

Page 27

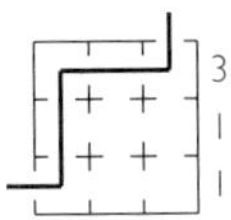

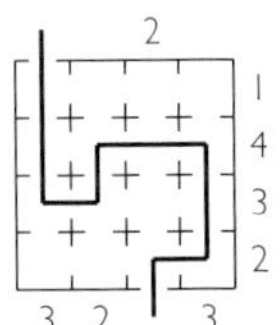

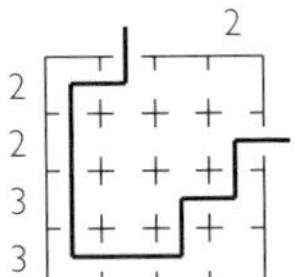

Page 29

LEVEL: 2

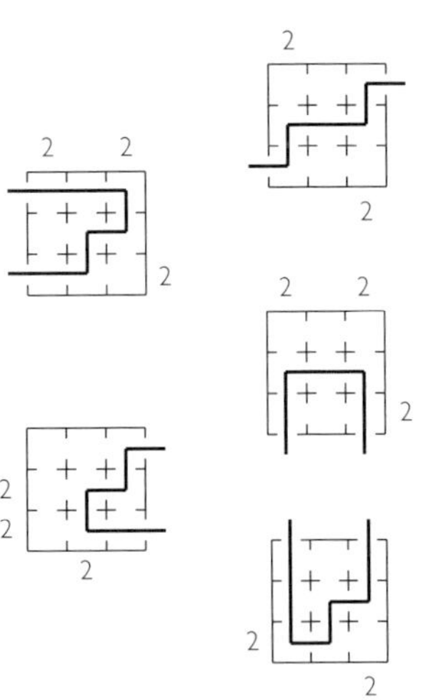

LEVEL: 2 (continued)

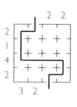

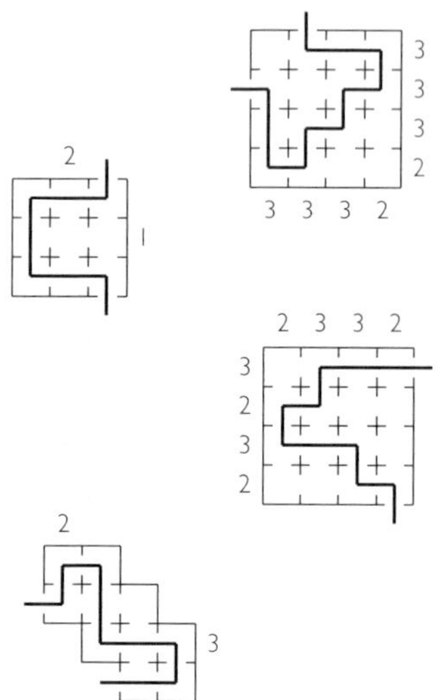

Page 30

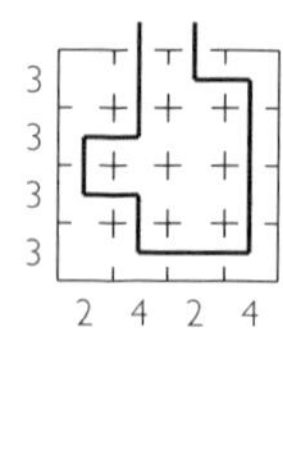

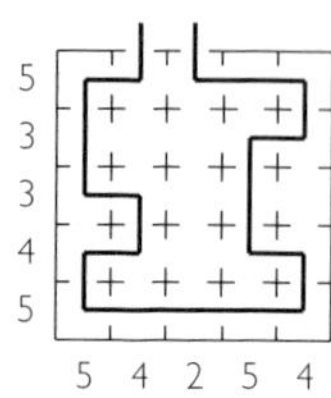

Page 31

Page 33

LEVEL: 3

Page 34

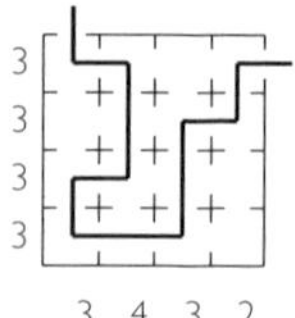

LEVEL: 3 (continued)

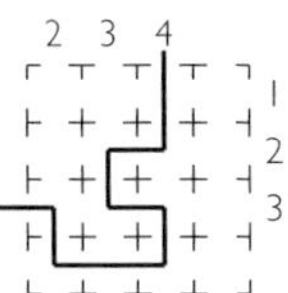

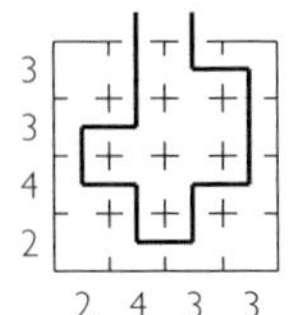

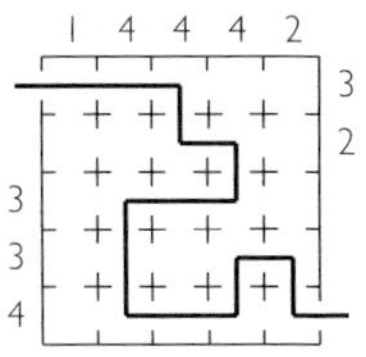

Page 35

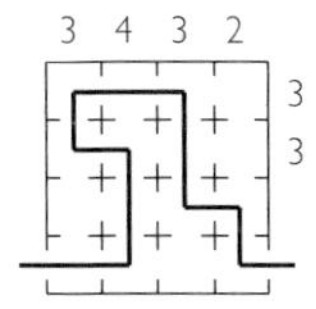

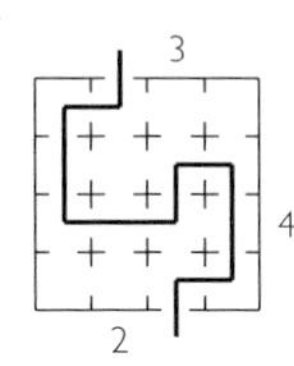

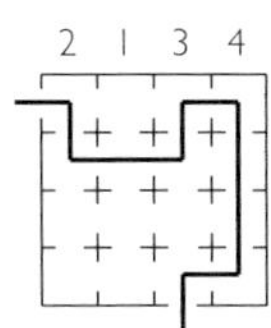

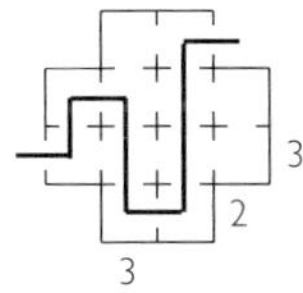

Page 36

Page 37

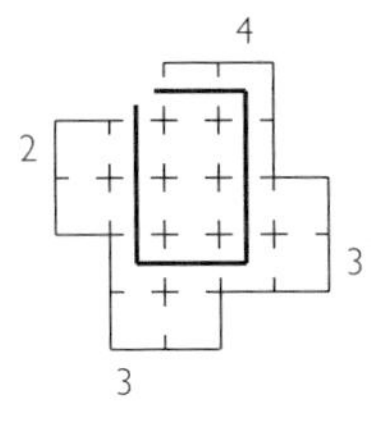

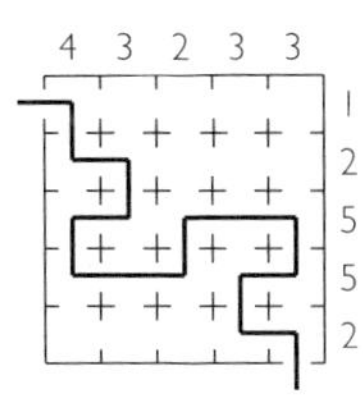

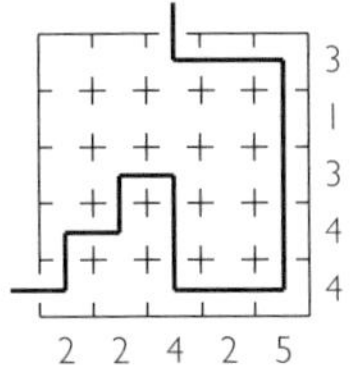

Page 39

LEVEL: 4

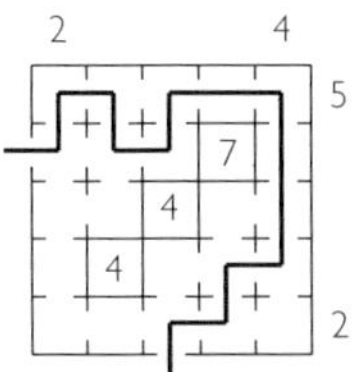

2 4
5
7
4
4
2

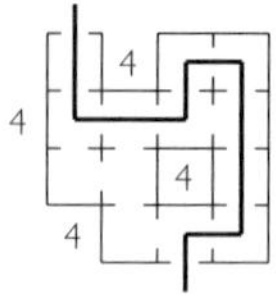

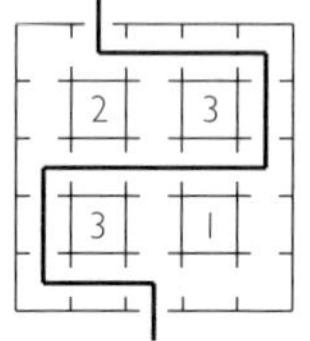

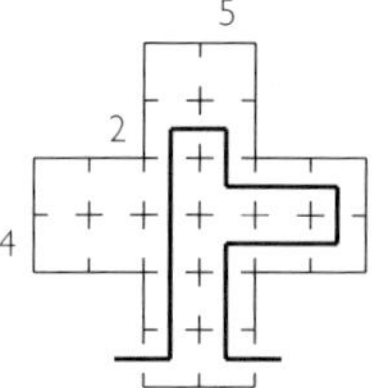

Page 40

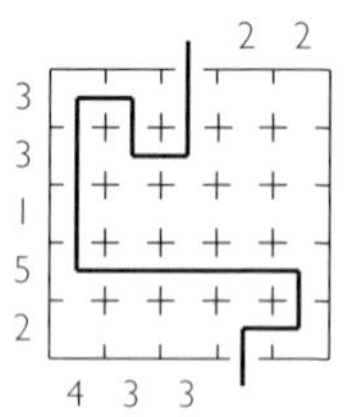

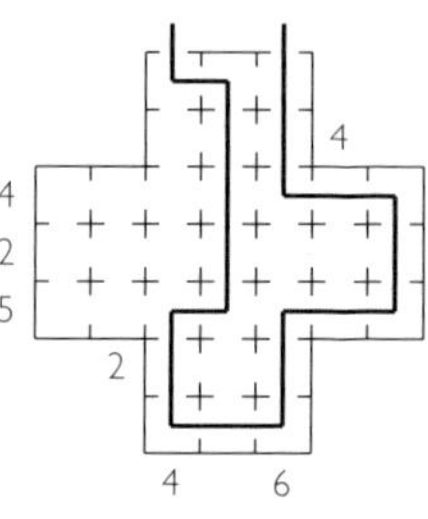

Page 41

Page 42

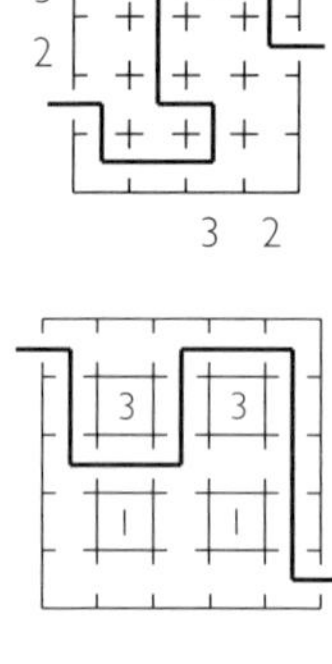

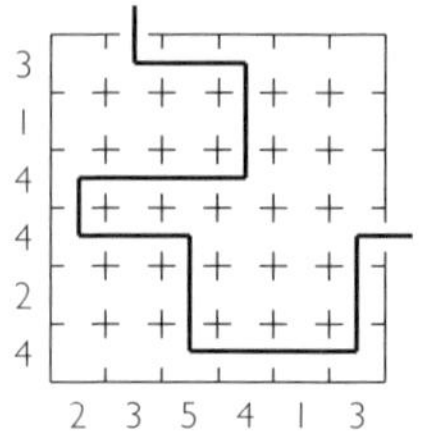

Page 43

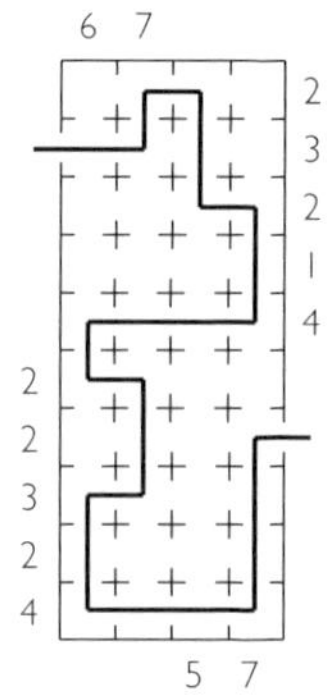

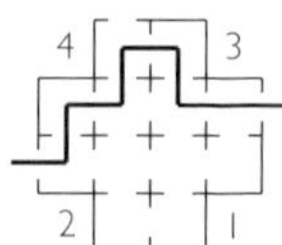

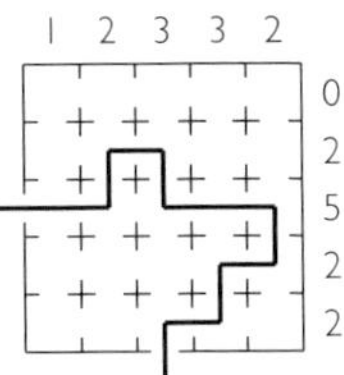

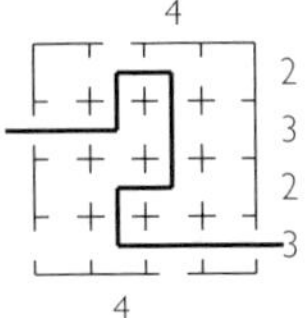

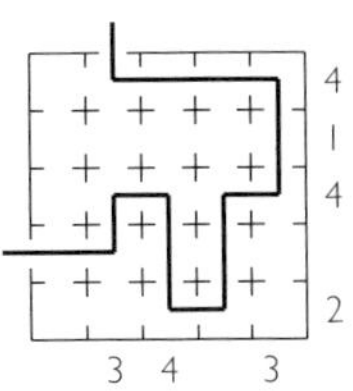

Page 44

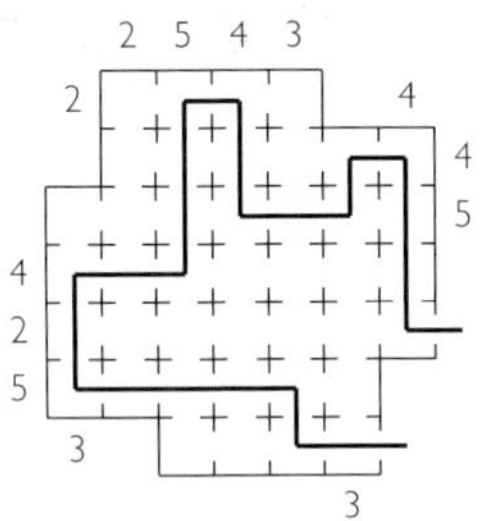

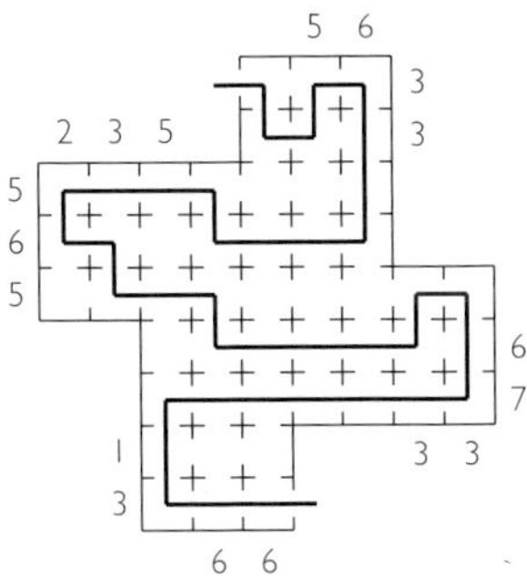

Page 45

Page 46

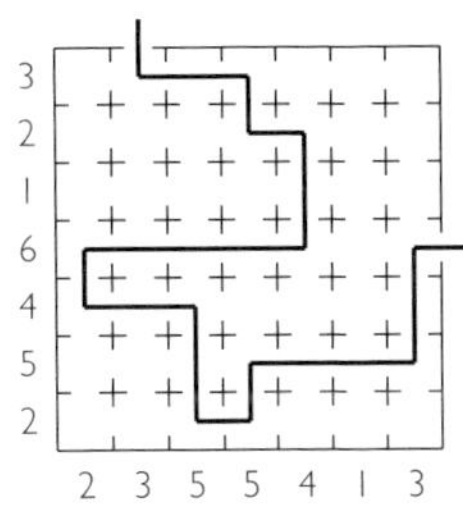

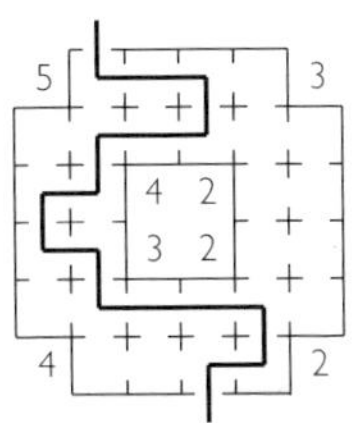

Page 47

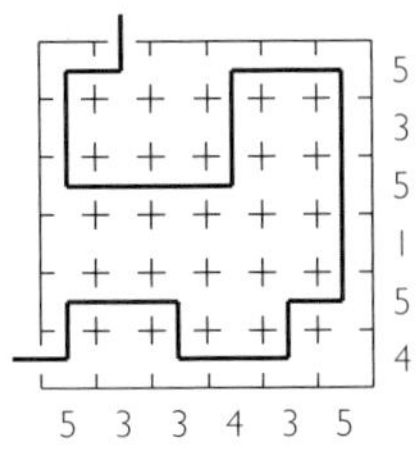

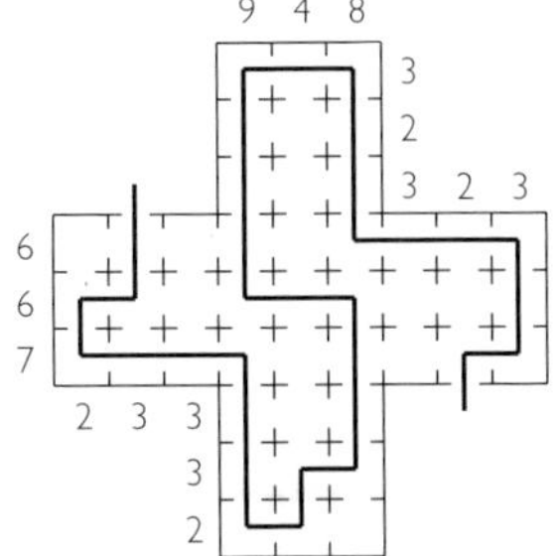

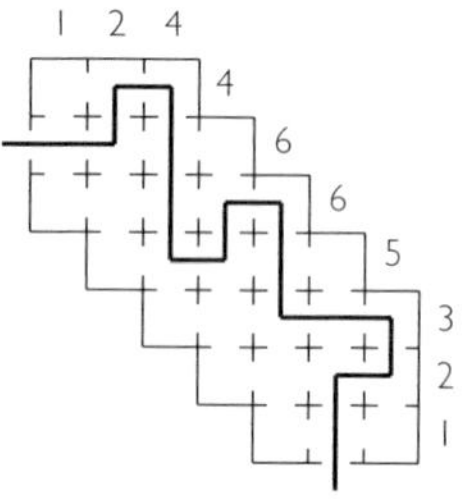

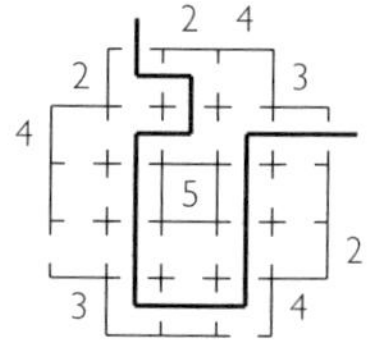

Page 48

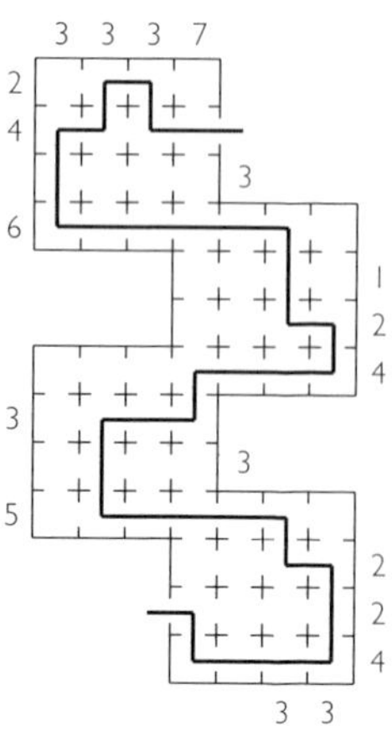

Page 49

Page 51

LEVEL: 5

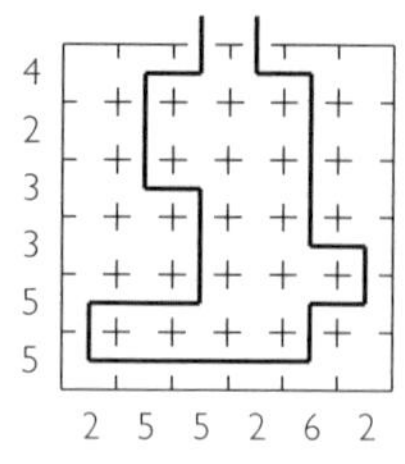

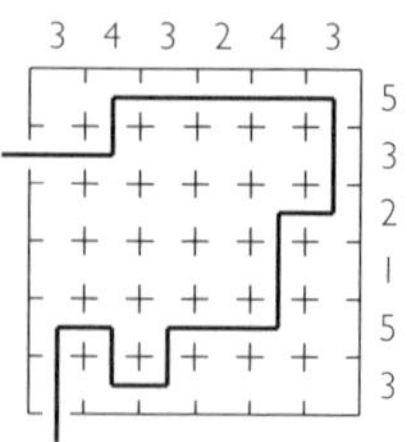

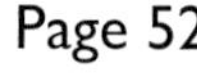

Page 52

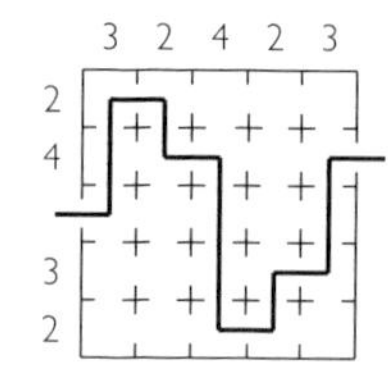

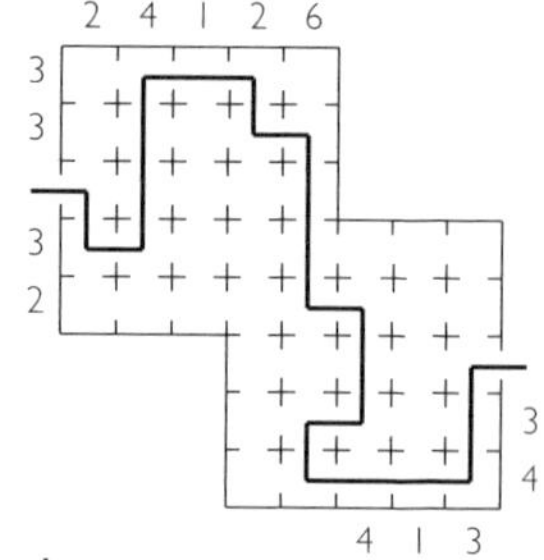

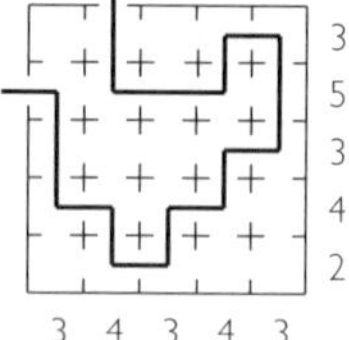

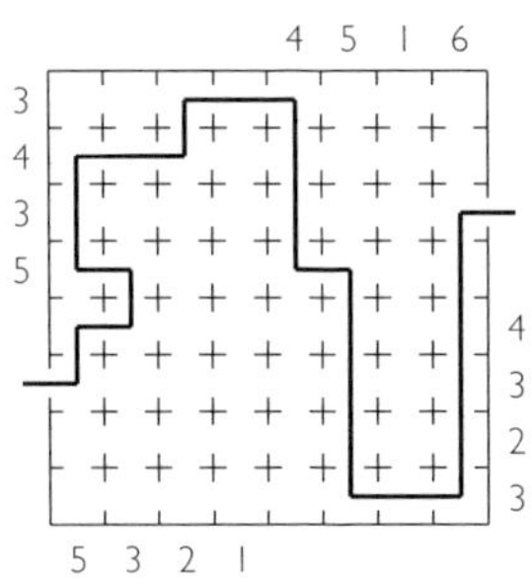

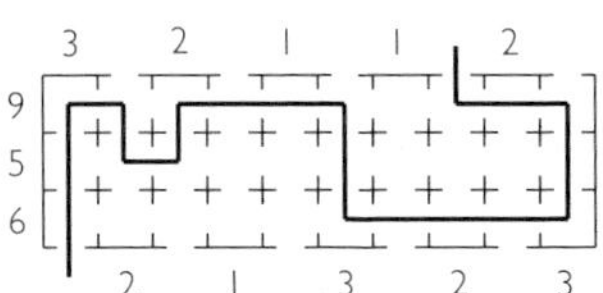

Page 53

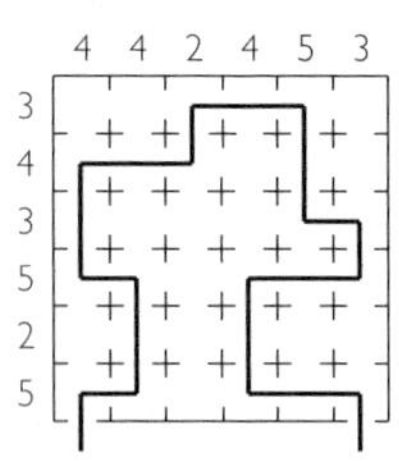

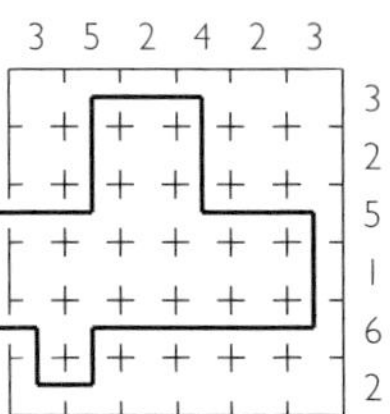

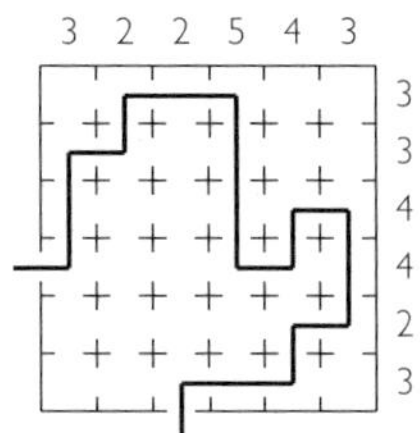

Page 54

Page 55

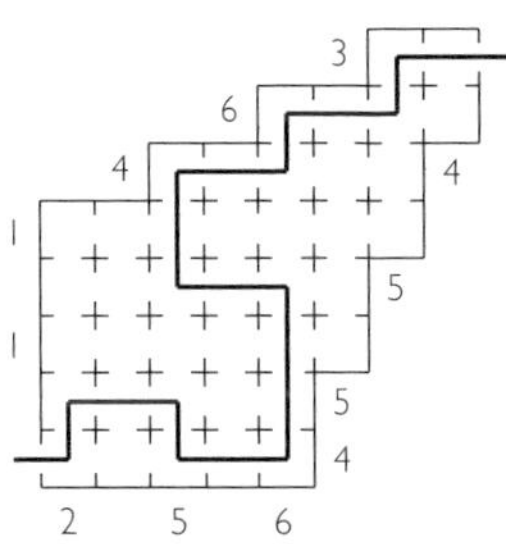

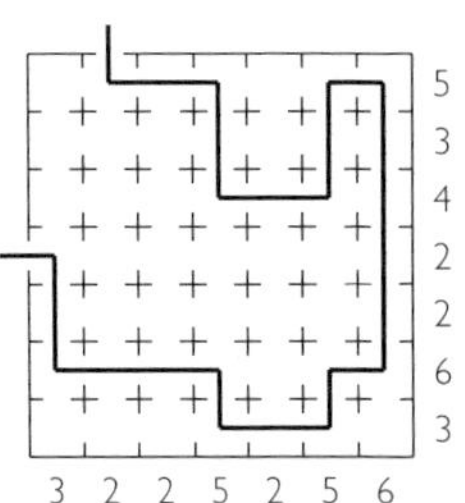

Page 56

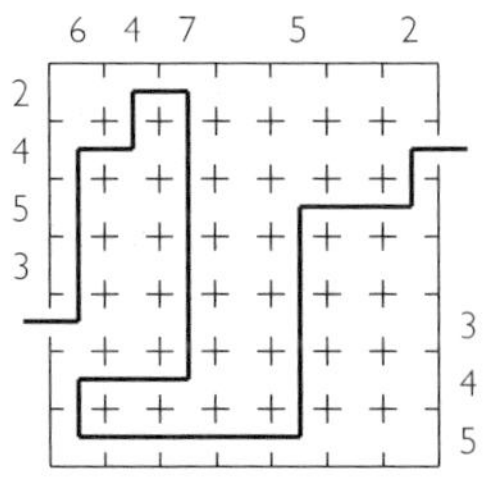

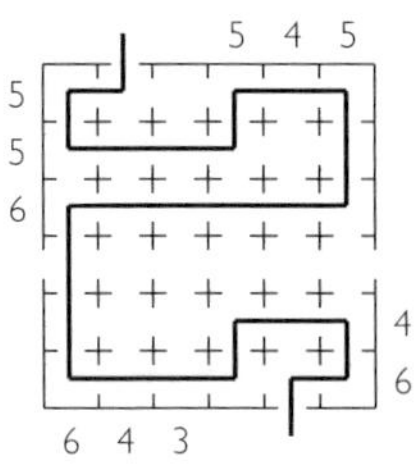

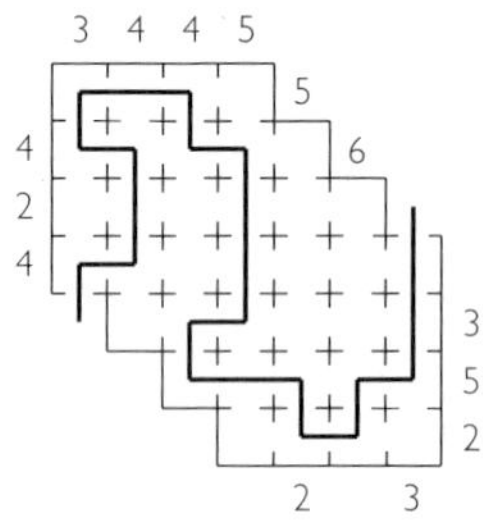

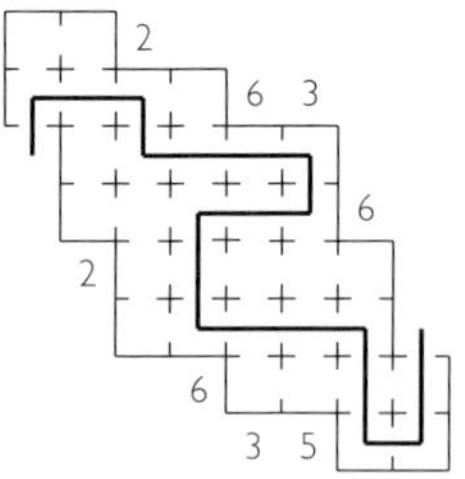

Page 57

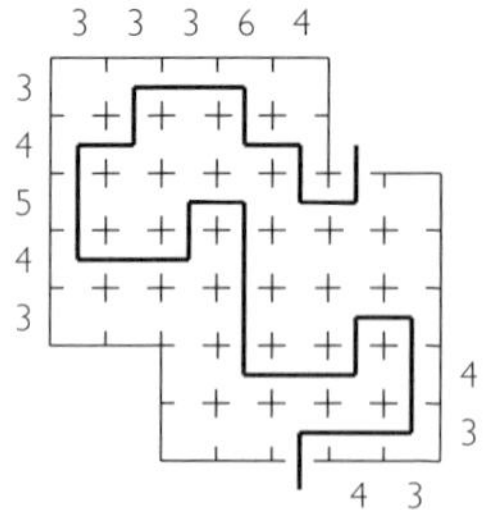

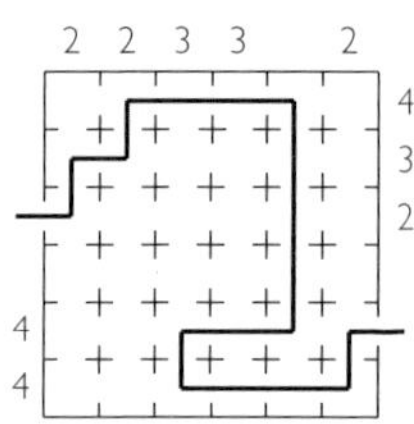

Page 58

Page 59

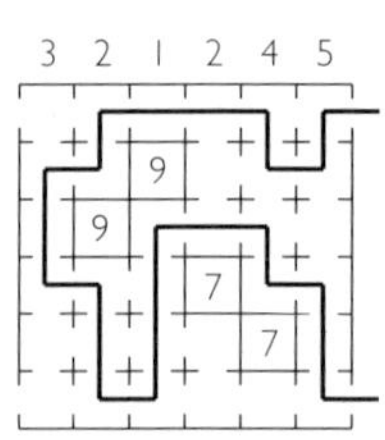

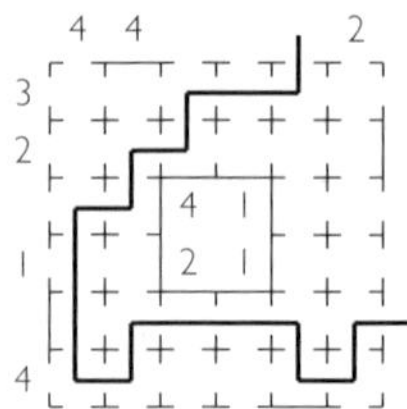

Page 60

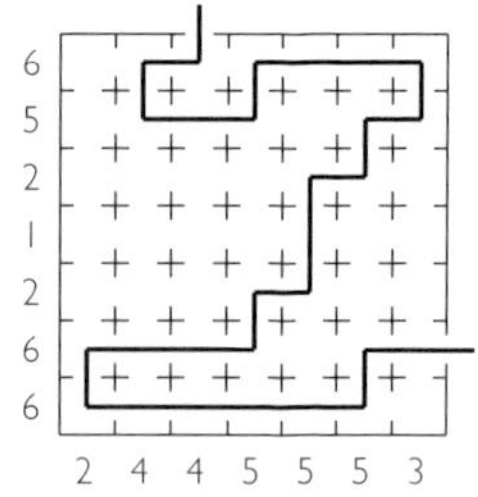

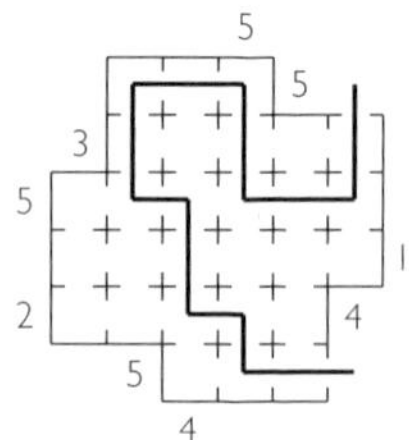

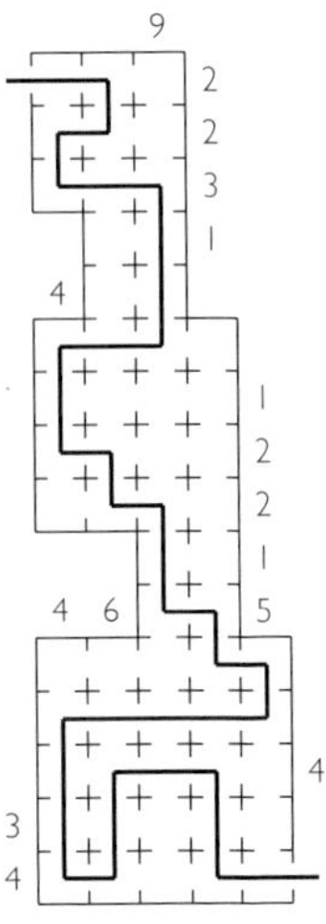

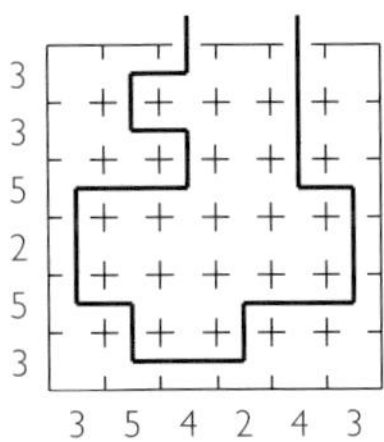

Page 61

Page 63

Page 64

Page 65

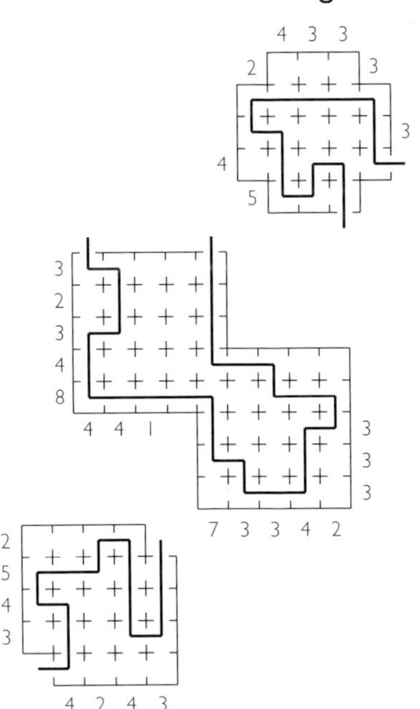

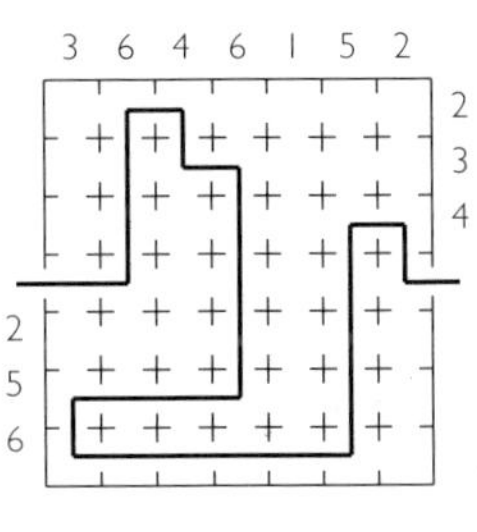

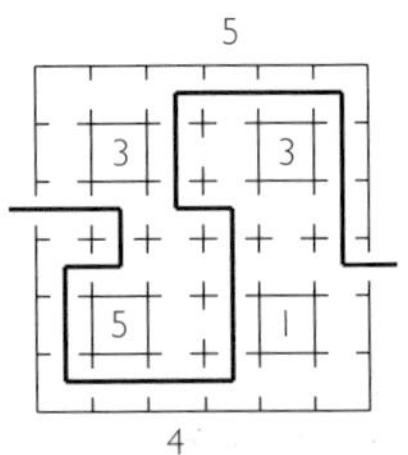

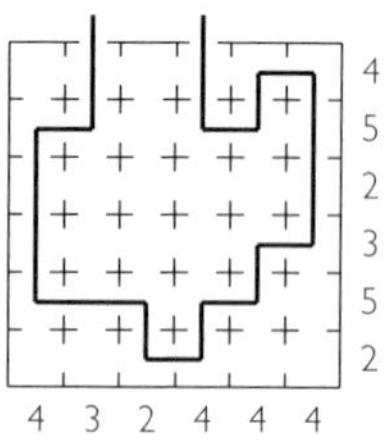

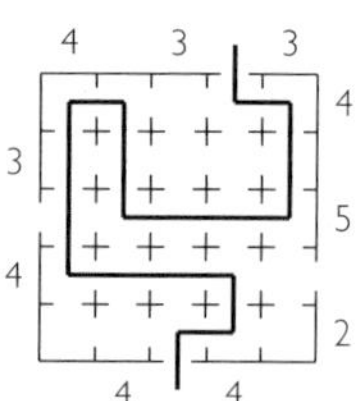

Page 66

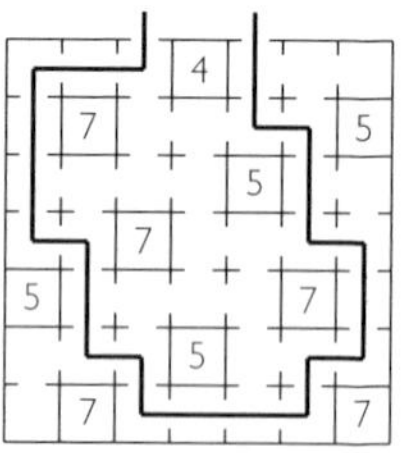

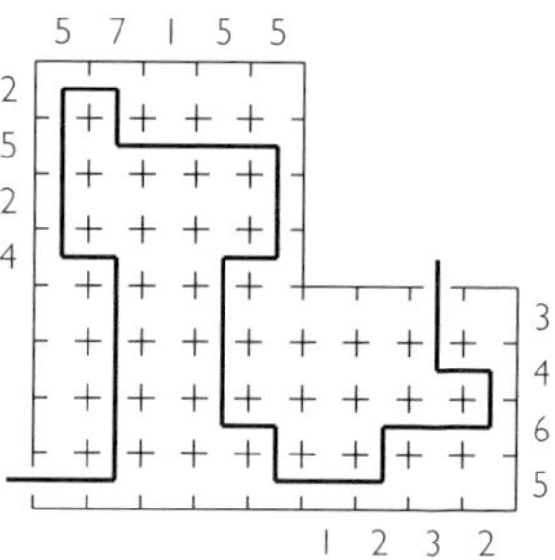

Page 67

Page 68

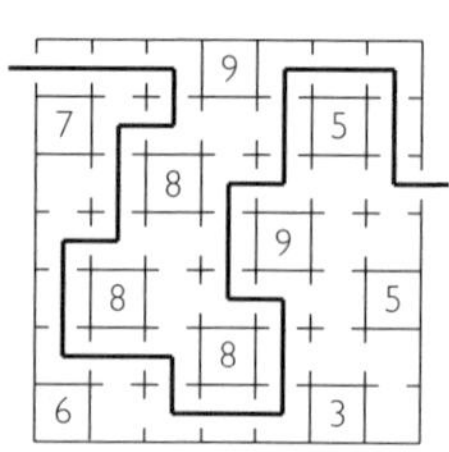

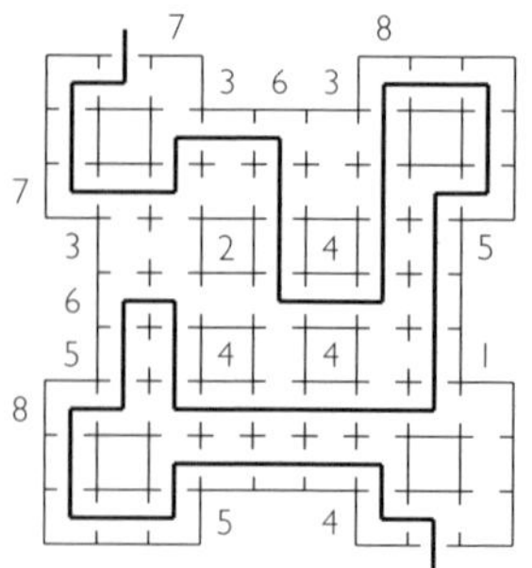

Page 69

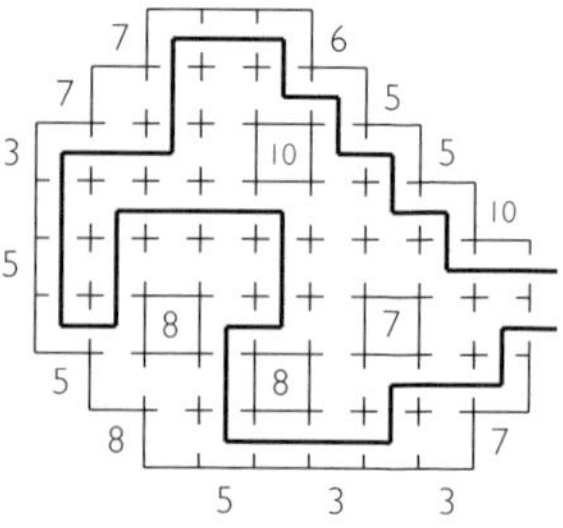

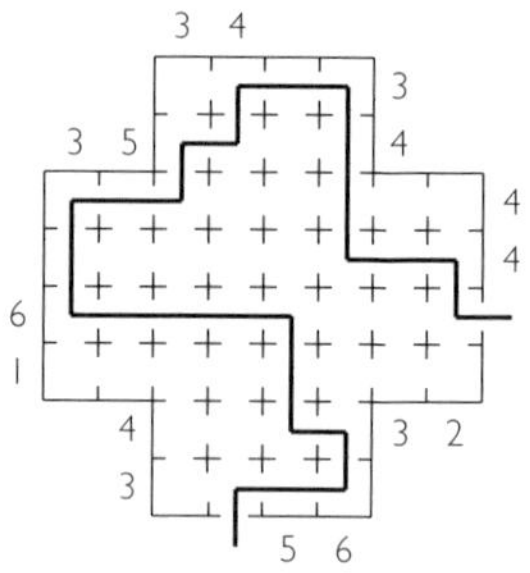

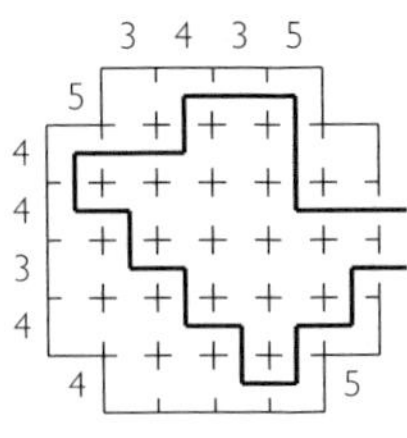
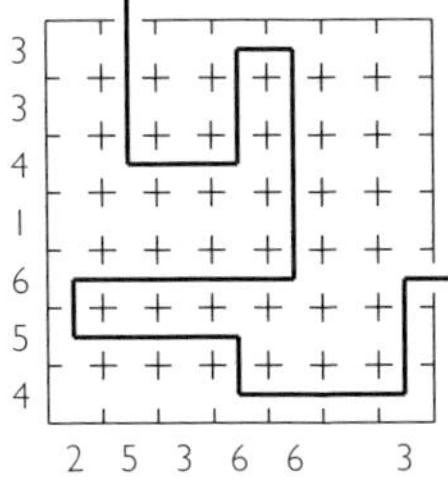

Page 71

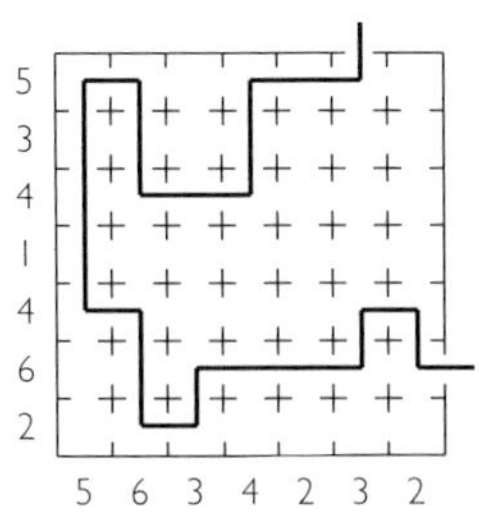
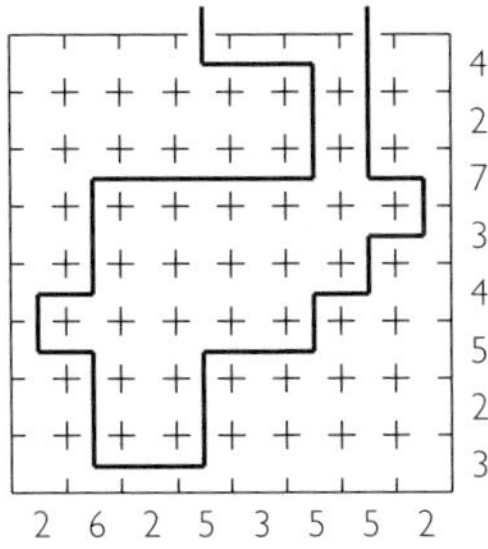

Page 72

Page 73

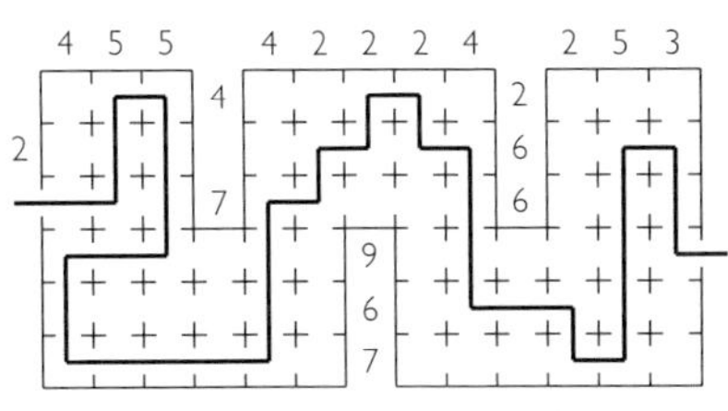
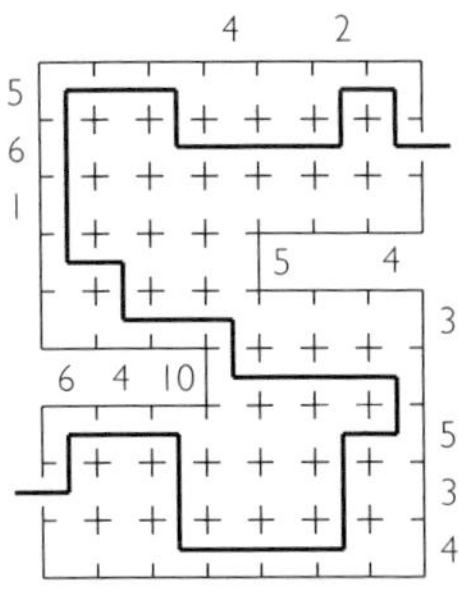

Page 74

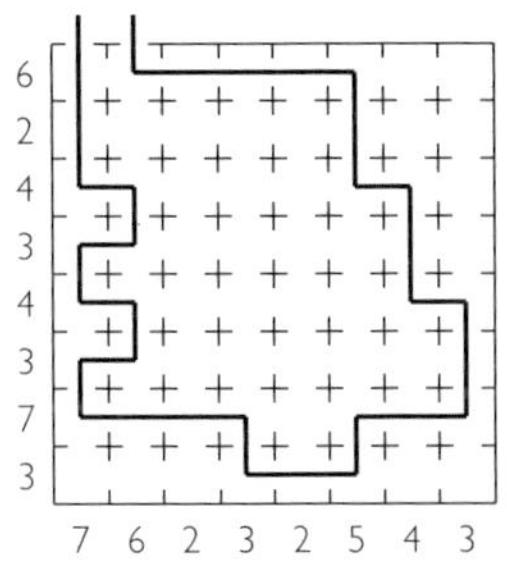
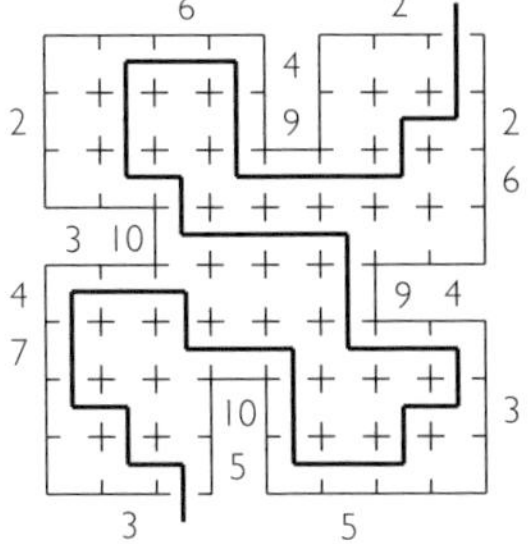

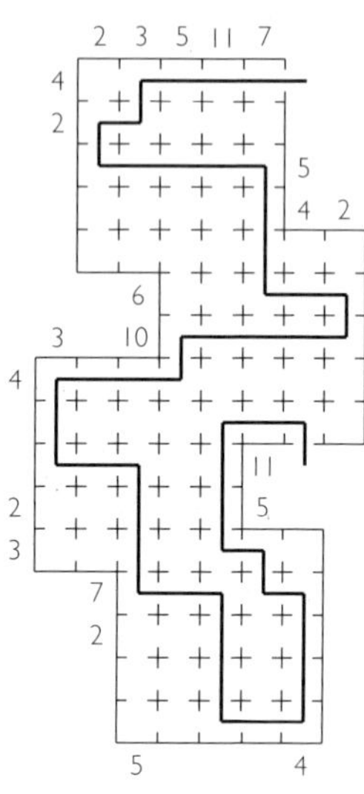

Page 75

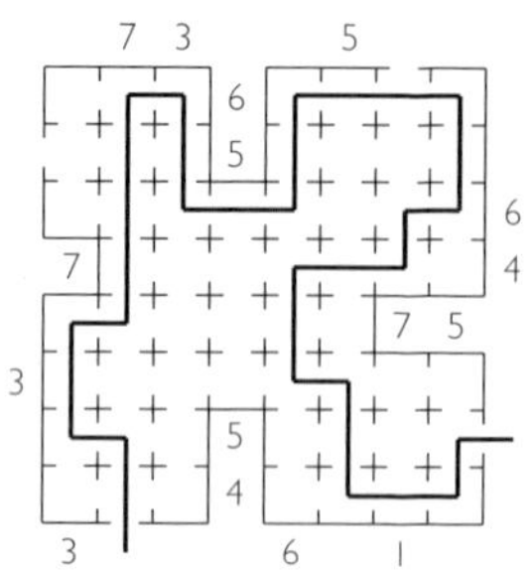

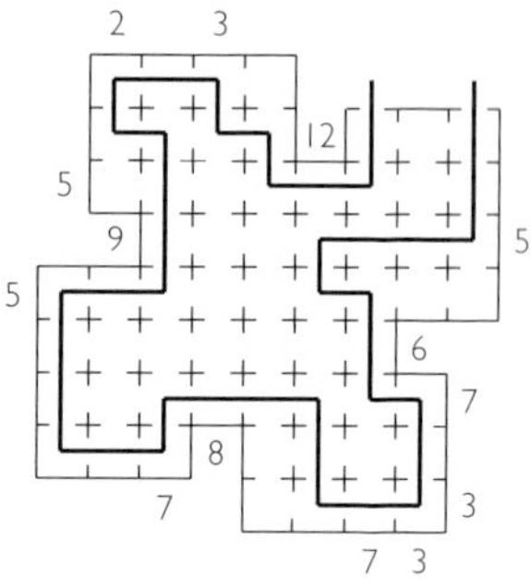

Page 76

Page 77

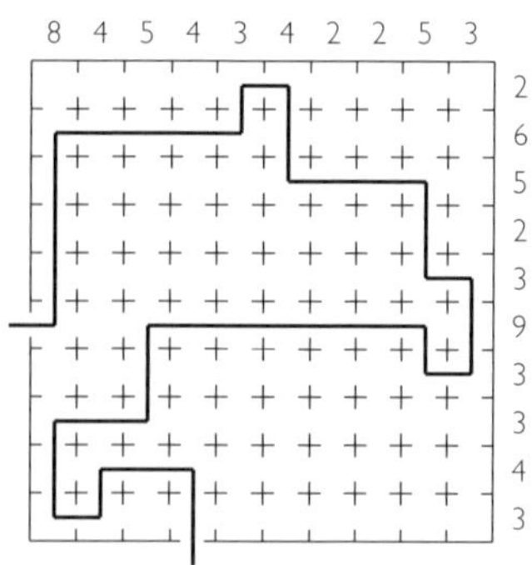

Page 78

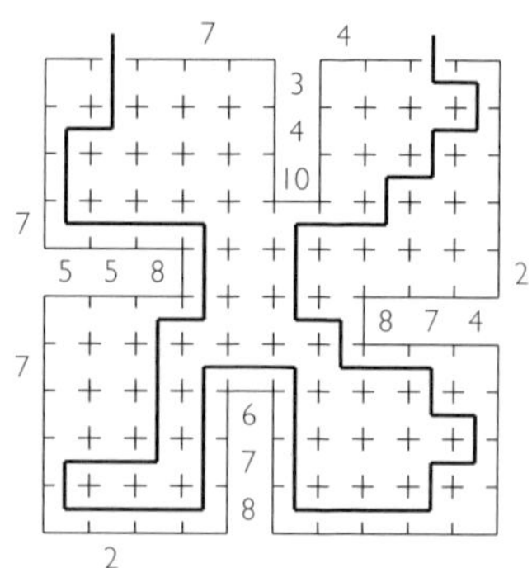

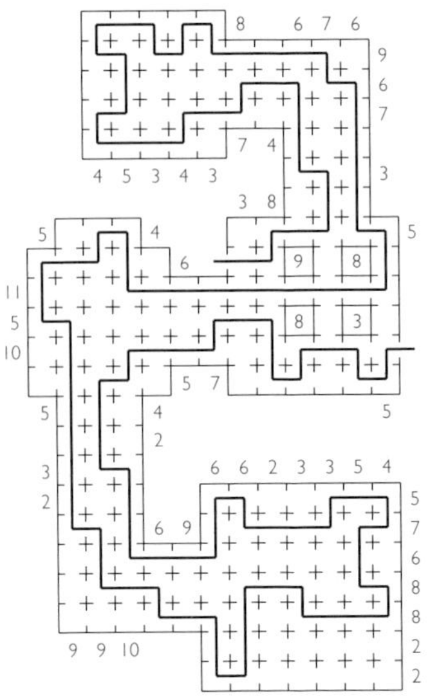

Page 79

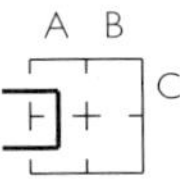

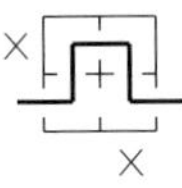

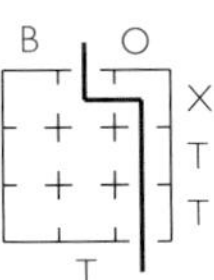

Page 82

Page 83

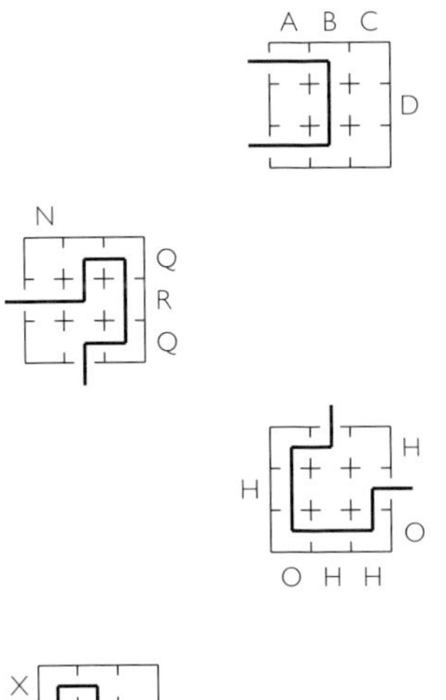

Page 84

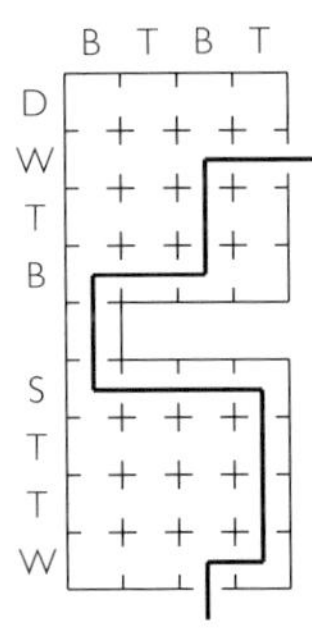

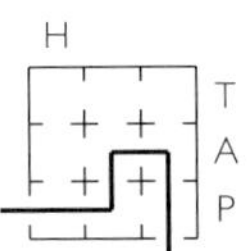

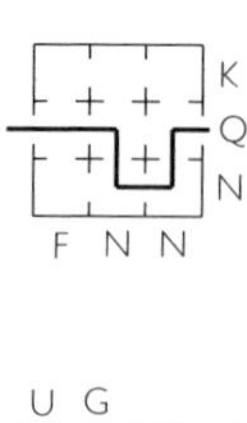

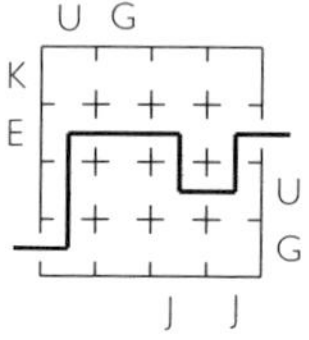

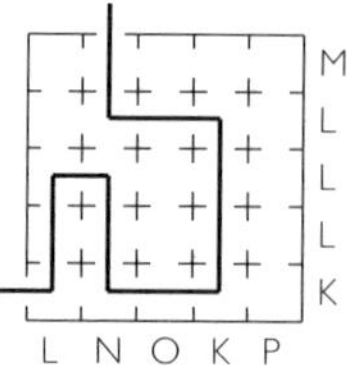

Page 85

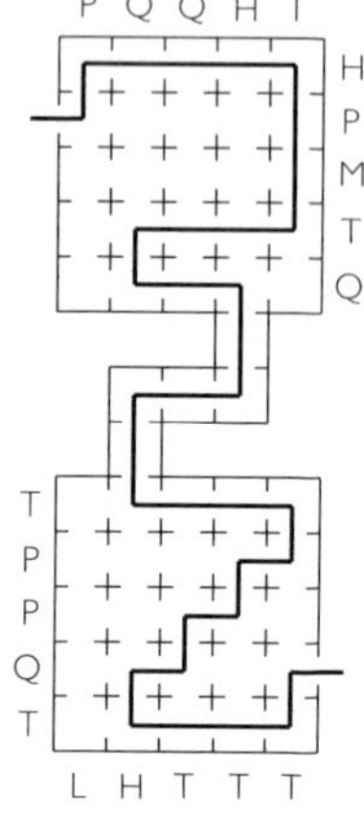

Page 86

For more, or to download the Path Puzzle app, please visit
www.pathpuzzles.com

Roderick Kimball was born in BC, making him either ridiculously old, or simply Canadian. In his youth, Roderick was sometimes spotted on the slow end of a soccer pitch but more often on the fast end of a chess board. (Surely you've heard of the notorious Kimball maneuver, in which one opens a chess match by flipping the king's pawn into the air such that it lands, butter side up, on the king's fourth rank.) A curious child, Rod once temporarily blinded himself by connecting his top and bottom braces with a 9-volt battery.

These days, Rod tours the world juggling with the Flying Karamazov Brothers and works at the National Museum of Mathematics. He is proud to say that his ancestry includes two very great grandmothers who were executed as witches and he once made bottled water come out Rosie O'Donnel's nose.